BEing

The Architecture of Experience

Yos Marél

BEing: The Architecture of Experience
BEing, Book I

Publisher's Note
The content of this book is intended for informational and self-discovery purposes only. It offers conceptual frameworks for self-inquiry, awareness, and perspective-taking. It is not intended to substitute for professional medical, psychological, legal, or therapeutic advice, diagnosis, or treatment.

This book does not establish a provider-patient, therapist-client, or coach-client relationship. The concepts discussed regarding the Four Channels of Experience (Body, Mind, Heart, and Spirit) are awareness-based models, not clinical interventions. If you are experiencing medical or psychological distress, please consult a qualified physician or licensed mental health professional.

To the fullest extent permitted by law, the author and publisher disclaim liability for damages or adverse outcomes arising from the use, interpretation, or application of the information contained in this book. Nothing in this disclaimer is intended to exclude or limit liability where such exclusion or limitation would be unlawful under applicable consumer protection laws.

Note on Personal Narratives
This book is a work of non-fiction. Personal stories and anecdotes are included to illustrate concepts and lived experience. While these accounts are true to the author's experience, some names, timelines, and identifying details may have been changed to protect the privacy of individuals involved.

References to other books, articles, websites, or external resources are provided for informational purposes only and do not constitute endorsement. All links and resources were accurate at the time of publication but may change over time.

Published by Synaria Fae
Visit the author at: www.yosmarel.com
Design and Layout: Iván Correa
ISBN (paperback): 979-8-9945372-0-6
ISBN (epub): 979-8-9945372-1-3
Printed in the United States of America
First Edition: February 2026

Contents

To Milo,
You did not just share with me unconditional love—you embody it. I have and will always love you.

To OO | AA,
Through the highs and lows, you gifted me unconditional and true friendship.

To my family,
Through every season, you remained present and caring. Even when I hid. Even when I believed I had nothing left to give.

With all of me,
Thank you.

Preface

Flow of Existence: From Pure Possibility to Creation/Manifestation

Welcome, fellow traveler. As we embark on our journey, let me share a friendly roadmap, the backbone of the proposition I named the *Flow of Existence*—a blueprint from the spark of possibility all the way to your every intended experience. In doing so, I invite you to exercise your imagination to co-create a field of understanding. We will use a language of exploration, where terms are not deterministic, without insisting on beliefs or challenging positions.

Consider every *experience*—every word you speak, every choice you make, every emotion you feel—as a form of *creation* that occurs within you. Your perceived reality is being crafted from the inside out, whether you realize it or not. This book will guide you in fine-tuning the creative process, so the life you experience more closely matches the one you consciously choose.

You'll see hints of the Flow of Existence's stages throughout the chapters. Whenever you wonder, "Why is the author talking about *tuning* my inner faculties?" or terms like "manifesting" or "awareness," remember this roadmap, knowing that each idea will make sense within this flow. This process unfolds in seven natural stages:

1. **Pure Possibility** (*e.g., raw potential, fundamental field, non-dual source*): Think of this as an open canvas or a clean slate. It's simply the space where anything can arise before you have chosen a color or brushstroke.

2. **I Am** (*e.g., self-presence, core awareness, consciousness, the soul's "I"*): From that open canvas, your sense of "I exist" emerges. This personal *self-presence* is the starting point for everything you do.
3. **Intention** (*e.g., wish, desire, goal, purpose*): From *I Am*, you ask yourself, "What do I want to experience?" or "Where do I want to be?" This clear, foundational expression of *will* becomes your guiding force for every next step.
4. **Faculties** (*e.g., your inherent capacities, built-in strengths, inner tuners*): You have built-in faculties, such as Will, Worthiness, and Wisdom, that you can adjust. Tuning these helps you shape and refine the raw energy expressed by your intention.
5. **Perspective & Attention** (*e.g., your lens, mindset, viewpoint, selective focus, aim*): I present these as one deeply linked stage. How you perceive and see things colors every decision. Widening or clearing your lens makes more possibilities visible. With *Intention* and *Faculties* aligned, you decide precisely where to place your *Attention*, collapsing possibilities down to a singular focus.
6. **Creation/Manifestation** (*e.g., formed experience, realized outcome, lived result, what shows up*): Your energy comes together into an outcome—an idea spoken, a project completed, a new habit formed. This *manifestation* is the moment potential becomes a tangible reality, a *creation*.
7. **Feedback Loop** (*e.g., course-correction, real-time calibration, re-tuning*): Every experience, whether it matches your plan or surprises you, is useful information. It shows you where to tweak your *Intention*, *Faculties*, *Perspective* (lens), or *Attention* (focus) next time.

Use the term that feels natural—whether you speak of "infinite potential," "inner aim," or "course-correction." While the names may differ, the underlying flow remains constant. Consider this preface your warm-up, a brief look at the creative rhythm you'll explore more deeply in every chapter. Remember:

It is not about learning how to manifest (you already do). It's about refining the quality of what you experience.

Note: This journey continues beyond these pages.

To support your exploration, you have access to a collection of free companion resources created specifically for readers of this book. These guides offer a deeper dive into the book's frameworks, including:

- *Expanded practices and real-world examples connected to each chapter*
- *The full, multi-perspective Glossary of Terms*
- *Periodic updates and new companion resources as they're released*

Visit www.yosmarel.com/book-resources to confirm your purchase and access the reader companion library.

Overture

Have you ever paused in the middle of your everyday life and felt, deep inside, that there is more to who you are? More than what you've experienced. More than what others have told you. Perhaps it happens in those rare moments of silence, amidst nature's stillness, in the unexpected disruption of your routine, or during seasons of unrelenting storms, bringing with them a fleeting realization that amidst the layers of roles and inherited stories you've chosen to hold, there is something more to life.

This book began at such a moment for me as I stood in the thin mountain air of a remote village, surrounded by a way of life profoundly different from mine. It was there, stripped of familiar comforts and identities, that I faced an unexpected realization: freedom wasn't something to be gained; it was something I had not yet recognized. It was always mine, hidden beneath illusions I had embraced without knowing.

What if life is less about *becoming* and more about *being*? What if the unimpeded expression of inner freedom flows already, but by simply welcoming and expanding awareness of raw potential, every experience is reconfigurable—shedding illusions and unfettering the free, authentic "you" beneath the accumulated noise?

My journey—and now, our shared space of exploration—moves outside the bounds of conventional wisdom. This book moves beyond transforming into *someone new* or *fixing* what feels broken. It offers compassionate and powerful reminders, clearing illusions that influence your authentic expression.

Together, we will explore three stages on this inward journey. First, we'll review essential *Threshold Keys*, pivotal insights—keys designed to unlock gateways within you, and introduce the *4-S Process* (*Self-Discovery*, *Self-Development*, *Self-Mastery*, and *Self-Knowledge*), engaging with a practical, experience-based framework for navigating your inner landscape. Next, we'll deepen awareness through *Seven Foundational Pillars*, and finally, we'll explore *Seven Faculties of Human Potential*—inherent qualities of your very essence, ready to be tuned as you consciously design experience and intended outcomes.

Why this exploration matters is simple yet profound: your life is too precious to be lived as a diminished version of yourself. The world is calling for you to live wholly expressed. You cannot be anyone else; more importantly, who you truly are needs no mask or imitation.

So if this is the path you choose, let us begin this journey toward being, living from recognized inner freedom, expressing and manifesting from full potential, authenticity, and worth. Within this presence, your truest and fullest life awaits.

From One Traveler to Another

Before we move deeper into this journey of awareness, there's something I will share with you.

During a visit to two of the four tribes of the Sierra Nevada in northern Colombia, a people whose wisdom flows poised through every gesture and silence, I asked a question that led to an unexpected reflection. One of the Mamos paused and looked at me for a moment before replying:

> *"When people visit us, they come to teach us. But we have not asked to be taught. We already know the way of Younger Brother."*

These words, spoken from poised wisdom, were delivered with kindness—a moment of clear recognition, free from harshness or confrontation. In that instant, I understood the difference between *teaching* and *sharing*.

Teaching, in many contexts, implies hierarchy. It often presumes that one person holds the truth and another does not. Even with the best intentions, teaching can carry a subtle residue of imbalance, the feeling of "I know" and "you don't." Sharing, however, is different.

When we share, we offer insight without insistence. We speak from lived experience, not from doctrine. We open our palms and let the other receive whatever they are ready for—without demand, judgment, or the need to be right.

And so, everything that follows in this book is shared, not taught. You are free to take what resonates. Free to leave what does not. Free to let the meanings evolve in you as your own awareness unfolds. This book is offered as a conversation, a companionship, a tool.

Even when I use language that sounds instructional or resolved, know that it arises from observation and lived experience, offered with humility and without obligation. I do not claim absolute truths. I do not hold the only map. What I share are stories, reflections, and frameworks that have helped me—and others—clear the way for more conscious, free, and authentic expression. May they simply serve you on your way.

In the years before I finished writing this book, I read specialized texts, studied, investigated, and explored a broad spectrum of traditions, disciplines, philosophies, and schools of thought. I immersed myself in the work of seekers, scientists, teachers, mystics, and researchers from vastly different corners of human experience, and interviewed people from diverse walks of life. As a result, the concepts in this book are intentionally interwoven from multiple lenses. Some ideas may feel familiar. Others may sound new. Words may carry different interpretations and meanings, depending on who speaks them, where they come from, or how they are used.

Every subject, term, and structure in this book has been chosen with awareness and with the full recognition that some readers may feel the need to challenge terminology or framework. That's okay. In fact, that's healthy. I welcome this exploration, hoping you bring curiosity rather than the need to be right. I chose words grounded in questions about the nature of reality, structured by psychological insights, and illuminated by quantum-inspired and energetic metaphors, generally narrated in everyday, plain speak.

My sincere recommendation is this:

Keep an open mind.
Don't fixate on the differences.
Seek the similarities.
Let resonance guide your integration.

So as we now enter our formal exploration, where words, perception, and sense of self expand, remember: *Here, you are not positioned as a student, but as the primary experiencer.* ***And this is simply the sharing of one traveler to another*.**

PART I

Foundations of Awareness

The next two chapters offer insights and pathways for exploring the factors that shape your present experiences and for intentionally tuning your internal sense of direction. This is the groundwork for expanded awareness—and with it, actualizing your inner freedom to experience life from greater clarity, presence, and alignment.

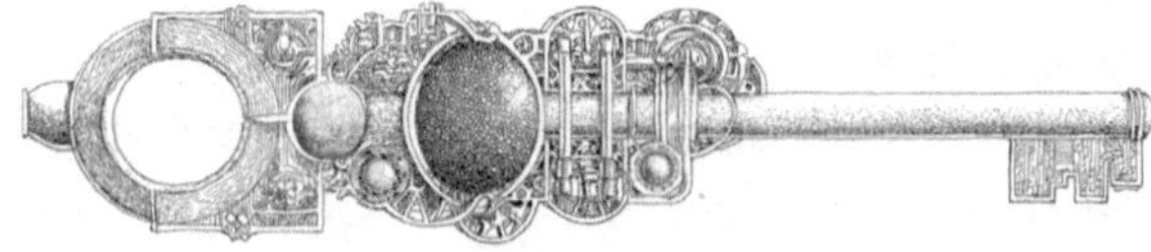

CHAPTER ONE

Threshold Keys

Unlocking Gateways

Imagine pausing at the threshold of a doorway you've passed countless times but didn't enter. It has always been there, blending into the familiar walls of your everyday life. This doorway doesn't lead outward but inward—into a room within your own being, of stored scripts, artifacts, costumes, and colorings held together by impermanent, illusory walls. Beyond them lies the field of Pure Possibility. Every creation and expression begins there, yet you keep shaping within rooms like these.

The keys to these inner doorways are not distant treasures. They are permissions to dissolve illusions, limiting stories, inherited scripts, and costumes you may have carried, reclaiming agency and authorship to create and design your every experience from pure potential. Each key unlocks a gateway from constraint to autonomy, from confusion to clarity—offered as a mirror, a decrypter, or a way to see more. Pause here, at the threshold. Take a breath. Step with presence.

1: You Are

It's unnecessary, and not possible, to *be* someone else. You aren't a project to be fixed or a self to be improved. You are whole and already carry everything you need.

> *Once you realize you are already whole, the pressure to measure up to anything external begins to dissolve.*

2: Perfect Nor Imperfect

Consider perfection as an ever-shifting idea borrowed from elsewhere. Release the concepts of "perfect" and "imperfect." You simply *are*, and that is enough.

> *When perfection is no longer the measure, worthiness doesn't need to be earned—it is known.*

3: Worthiness is Intrinsic

Beliefs are a pre-intention, a chosen filter that pre-sets and conditions your experience. Consider worthiness not as a belief, but as intrinsic. You exist, so no filter is required.

> *From that awareness, inner freedom is clear.*

4: Freedom is Intrinsic

You are so free that you can choose your own constraints or release them. Inner freedom is not earned; it's actualized.

> *Freedom within allows for clear intention, guided by presence.*

5: Intention Beyond Hope

Intentions matter, yet they alone do not determine outcomes. Intention moves energy, but without coherence, it can disperse into mere longing.

> *Intention alone is not the current. Full power flows when intention partners with aligned will.*

6: Power of Will

Unrestricted power of will flows from the conscious alignment of worthiness, focused intent, and action. It flows unrestricted not from wondering if there is a way, but from knowing there is always a way.

> *Will shapes how reality takes form, and it begins in perception. Through will, aligned with awareness, possibility expands probability.*

7: Perception is Reality

Your perceived reality surfaces as you choose to frame it. Each moment is a snapshot, and every snapshot is an invitation to explore new configurations.

> *Language structures our perception; words are tools that construct your inner world.*

8: Words Do Matter

Words reveal and shape the way you perceive life. Each thought spoken and emotion named organizes your inner landscape. Speak consciously; words carry echoes far beyond sound.

> *Words don't always lead to truth. They may point, but they can never capture the whole.*

9: True Isn't Always Truth

Every viewpoint is like a facet of a crystal—each reveals something true, but never the whole. There is always more than one version of every story.

> *In the spaces between partial truths, love offers coherence—a force both restorative and expansive.*

10: Love *You* Too

Just as there is wisdom in rhythm and reciprocity, there is wisdom in love—as emotion, force, intention, state, or action—toward *yourself* and others.

> *To feel love fully, you may need to reclaim the source of your emotions as your own.*

11: Your Emotions Are Yours

Others cannot give you emotions or force them onto you; yet they may only reflect or trigger what is already present within. Your emotions arise from within.

> *To shift emotions, sometimes you must let go—compassionately and deliberately.*

12: Let Go to Flow

Forgiveness isn't giving up justice; it's entrusting yourself to a current that brings about opportunity and life.

> *Letting go opens unknown spaces, where courage bridges into possibility.*

13: Courage Invites Possibility

Consider courage not as the absence of fear, but as the steady openness and movement to meet possibility with presence as it arises.

> *With courage, awareness sharpens—illuminating the faculties already within you, ready to be tuned.*

14: Awareness is Key

As awareness expands, you recognize what already lives within you: Mastery, Awareness, Worthiness, Will, Wisdom, Oneness, and Creativity; inherent faculties, instruments in life's harmonic expression.

The fourteen keys you've just explored are shared as sparks—brief illuminations of what waits just beyond your current view. With each key, another illusion may loosen its hold, allowing your awareness to expand through compassionate undoing or willful reinforcement. This expansion reveals what has been present all along, stirring a recognition of false bindings and the choices, patterns, and whispers of wisdom that live within. We now turn our attention to four dimensions of conscious engagement: pathways for meeting yourself and navigating life through recognized inner freedom.

CHAPTER TWO

The 4-S Process

Self-Discovery, Self-Development, Self-Mastery, and Self-Knowledge

The *4-S Process* begins with the premises: *Freedom and worthiness are intrinsic*. Engaging with life from this awareness shifts the focus from striving to being. This chapter explores four interconnected dimensions of that engagement, each offering a unique way of exercising authority, authorship, and autonomy over your life experiences.

- **Self-Discovery** reveals what has always been present beneath conditioning.
- **Self-Development** empowers and equips you to shape your experiences with clear intention.
- **Self-Mastery** expresses awareness in real time.
- **Self-Knowledge** roots your experience in coherence, becoming your internal compass.

Consider these four dimensions as inner movements already alive within you.

Self-Discovery

Self-Discovery is the process of gaining insight into your own character, values, beliefs, and desires with compassion and honesty. It is about revealing the *who* beyond societal expectations. This means recognizing the external beliefs and narratives that may have distorted your authentic expression. By becoming aware of these layers, you reclaim authority, rooted in your core *I Am* presence—the unconditioned sense of being that underlies experience. This journey is about potentializing the free flow from your authentic self, the genuine expression beyond roles or conditioning; it invites you to see *what is*, instead of striving to become a different version of yourself built on conditioned assumptions. **Through Self-Discovery, you discover what to keep or release**.

Self-Development

Self-Development is the deliberate process of tuning your inherent faculties—the capacities you already carry (we will explore these further in Part III) to develop from what you have discovered. Unlike Self-Discovery, which reveals what is, **Self-Development equips**; it is an active expression of your authorship and autonomy, leveraging your tuned faculties to craft experiences from raw potential and with focused intent. Each encounter then becomes an opportunity for adaptive learning, feeding data back into your tuning loop so you continuously refine how your faculties engage.

Self-Mastery

Self-Mastery is the ongoing practice toward living in conscious alignment with your authentic self's potential. It arises from deeper awareness and the willingness to meet each moment with embodied presence and passion. Whereas Self-Discovery reveals and Self-Development equips, **Self-Mastery is where awareness becomes lived in real-time**. It expresses embodied expertise, refinement, authority, and the choice to respond rather than react out of mere instinct or habit. As you become more conscious of how and why you choose, you express and design experiences with alignment and coherence.

Self-Knowledge

Self-Knowledge is the *lived understanding of who you are* and what, why, how, when, and where you are experiencing. It is not simply the accumulation of insight, but the integration of all you've discovered, developed, and mastered into a coherent sense of being. Where Self-Discovery reveals, Self-Development equips, and Self-Mastery lives in real-time, **Self-Knowledge roots from alignment**. It arises when what you know, feel, choose, and do resonate in harmony. This integration brings depth to your sense of self as a coherent presence. Lived alignment is steady integrity—walking in step with your authentic self's unconditioned expression. As circumstances shift, Self-Knowledge allows you to navigate adjustment without losing your center, trusting your internal compass rather than external validation.

PART II

Expanding Awareness
Seven Foundational Pillars

Having established a framework for living with an unfiltered sense of inner-freedom with the Threshold Keys and the 4-S Process, we now deepen our exploration. This part of our journey is dedicated to seven foundational pillars of awareness—the core understandings that empower you to consciously engage with your own self-discovery, development, mastery, and knowledge.

Our exploration continues with the principle that **Words Do Matter**, for the architecture of the language we use actively shapes our reality. From there, we will explore the nature of **I Am**, recognizing the core of your being that exists beneath transient identities. We will then examine the dynamic interplay of **Duality and Polarity**, discerning the spectrum beyond rigid opposites into a more nuanced existence. This leads us to **Framing Your Reality**, understanding how your unique perceptions construct your world.

Building on this, we will deconstruct **Beliefs**, questioning inherited narratives to reclaim your creative freedom. To integrate these insights, we will map what I refer to as the four **Channels of Experience**—Body, Mind, Heart, and Spirit (attention + intention) — the active interfaces that receive and shape physical sensation, meaning-making, emotional resonance, and directed focus. Body, Mind, Heart, and Spirit (attention + intention) aren't anatomical references so much as symbolic terms used to represent the channels. While each will be explored in Chapter 8, a quick note on Spirit: here it refers to the interplay of attention and intention, the vector that continually directs your experience—whether consciously or not. Finally, we'll introduce the concept of the **Faceted BEing**, balancing how you want to be seen, how others see you, how you see yourself, and who you authentically are.

Together, these seven foundations provide a comprehensive map of your inner landscape, empowering you to navigate your life with greater clarity, focused intent, and an expansive, liberated perspective. Let us continue.

CHAPTER THREE

Words Do Matter

Words are not mere tools of communication. They are instruments of construction—laying the scaffolding of thought, shaping the boundaries of perception, defining the architecture of our inner and outer worlds. Before any action arises, before identity is claimed or denied, a word has already been spoken, internally or aloud. With that word, the shaping begins.

The principle *Words Do Matter* serves to recognize a fundamental dynamic:

> *When unconscious, language becomes the architect of illusion; when conscious, it becomes a liberating force.*

Words do not merely carry meaning; they *make* meaning. They are vibrations etched into awareness, acting as both mirrors and weavers of reality. Every sentence you think or speak shapes the space in which you live.

Most of the language we use is inherited, spoken in rhythms passed down from family, culture, and belief systems. When we are unaware, language begins to *speak us*. We become fluent in stories that aren't ours and fluent in doubts handed down like heirlooms.

To reclaim authorship of your life, you must first reclaim authorship of your words. It isn't about polished speech or replacing one performance with another, but about recognizing language as a creative act. When your words are shaped by presence rather than programming, you stop echoing someone else's story and write your own.

Verbal Architecture: How Language Shapes Your Inner World

I once ran a small visual communications firm, helping clients express complex ideas with greater impact through clarity and design. Our focus was always on how to structure a message so it would land clearly and memorably—in a way that resonated with the audience. Looking back, I see how much of that intention mirrored a deeper pattern in me: shaping messages to gain acceptance as much as for creating understanding, aligning them with what others wanted to hear or what I believed they expected. Simultaneously, for 30 years I served as an ordained minister, speaking publicly multiple times a week—from small circles to large venues—applying learned rhetoric, refined delivery, and layered messages with carefully chosen metaphors. But the architecture of my words often came from scripts I had not questioned.

In the work and book *Teaching Physical Education*[1] by Muska Mosston and Sara Ashworth—which is more about teaching & learning and human development than just physical education—these brilliant lifelong educators, drawing from decades of research and deep respect for pedagogy, refer to *assessment* and *feedback* as aspects of *verbal behavior*.

Although their work was centered in pedagogy, it set me on a path to understanding something essential: choosing the right words is vital, and unlearning the inherited patterns behind them is a fascinating challenge. For example, differentiating between

---

1 Muska Mosston and Sara Ashworth, "The Role of Feedback in the Teaching-Learning Process," chap. 4 in *Teaching Physical Education*, 1st Online ed. (Spectrum Institute for Teaching and Learning, 2008), https://spectrumofteachingstyles.org/index.php?id=16

good and *bad*, *right* and *wrong*, and *correct* and *incorrect* makes a tremendous impact on how we define ourselves, our behavior, and our relationship with everyone and everything else. The words *good*, *bad*, *right*, and *wrong* pertain to values, morality, and ethics, while *correct* and *incorrect* are about accuracy and precision. If you say 1 + 2 = 4, it is simply incorrect, not *wrong* or *bad*. Shifting these words when formulating a statement makes an enormous difference.

During a long and disorienting depression I experienced, I began to apply these concepts inward, shifting focus to myself. This is how I began to shape what I now call *Verbal Architecture*—how we speak, the words we default to, and how the structure of our sentences reveals far more than we often notice. Even when our intentions are sincere, our phrasing can reinforce assumptions, blur meaning, or create dissonance between what we hope to express and what we actually say.

It was years after resigning from ministry that I realized many of the speaking patterns when preaching mirrored beliefs about myself I had adopted as identifying truths. Without realizing it, the very architecture of my words—the *how*, *what*, *when*, *where*, and a confused *why*—amplified feelings of fear, guilt, and unworthiness. Wrapped in traditions I hadn't yet questioned, my internal dialogue, and that of many I interacted with, was full of hidden architecture: subtle absolutes and layered judgments. "I'm not worthy!" "I'm right." "Hopefully I can be forgiven?" "That... them... it... made me feel this way." These constructions follow patterns chosen to adopt and internalize long before they are given conscious permission.

It didn't change overnight. But as I started noticing not just *what* I was saying to myself but *how*, *why*, *when*, and from *where*, I began to complement Self-Discovery with Self-Development. I started to shift from programmed direction to compassionate formulation, from a borrowed voice to authentic clarity. Expanded awareness reveals the hidden structure of how we speak. It allows us to reclaim authorship and autonomy over our choice of words. Verbal Architecture shapes how we locate ourselves in thought, emotion, action, and identity. It is a window into our beliefs, our perception of self, and the inner reality we've chosen to experience.

And we can shape that reality differently. Intentionally. Consciously. Freely.

Whether you're speaking aloud or silently within, your *Verbal Architecture* forms invisible blueprints. Some patterns are survival mechanisms; others are so normalized that you don't even hear them anymore. But they're there—and they're shaping the tone of your inner world. Notice how a subtle change in wording shifts both agency and trajectory:

- "I guess I'll try." to "I choose to begin."
- "I always screw this up." to "This is an area I'm learning to navigate."
- "They made me feel worthless." to "I felt worthless when I heard their words; they activated an old belief I'm ready to unlearn."

These revisions move speech from limitation or self-qualification toward choice, from global self-attack to authority and autonomy. Each phrase reveals alignment (or misalignment) between attention and intention. Speaking from lack often signals an attempt to fill a perceived void ("I need someone to validate me"). Speaking from sufficiency reflects a resourced, settled state from which generosity and compassion is easier ("I feel seen and I'd love to share this"). But don't weaponize "toxic positivity" to deny real deprivation or harm. Aim for accurate language over performative optimism.

Your relationship with the world hinges on how you experience enoughness and how you speak from it. Words are directional: between despair and hope lies articulation; between resentment and release lies reframing; between numbness and clarity lies tone. Verbal Architecture is *orientation*. **You don't need a new self—just a new sentence.**

Micro-practice (4 steps):

Observe: "They said X." Then acknowledge: "I feel hurt." Then name the belief: "It poked the 'not enough' story." Then choose: "I'm practicing a new script and setting a boundary."

Words in the Flow of Existence

Words Do Matter can be understood as a powerful energetic tool that influences how we filter and transform our experiences, particularly through its impact on the *Perspective & Attention* stages of the *Flow of Existence*. Words are not merely symbols or sounds; they influence our inner interpretative filter—our *Perspective*. As this perspective shifts in response to the words we choose, our field of probable experiences expands or contracts, allowing or disallowing emotions—those that might have previously been filtered out—to enter into our *Attention*. In this way, words recalibrate the interpretive field and help expand awareness. They make new possibilities available—or narrow the field—depending on the precision and resonance of language.

The words we choose also direct our *Attention*. For example, when we consciously select words that resonate with openness or insight, we direct our Attention towards those qualities. This selective focus not only determines the immediate *Manifestation* but also feeds the *Feedback Loop*—progressively aligning our *Faculties* and refining our *Perspective*.

Words carry intention. When we articulate intention with clarity, we impose a directed modulation on our internal field. Our *Faculties* interpret and integrate them into lived experience. In this way, words become the vehicles for transmitting and reinforcing conscious choice.

> ***Note:*** *In Chapter 9 we'll return to explore how Feedback becomes a verbal art—choosing words that course-correct during the Flow of Existence.*

Language in the 4-S Process

Conscious language becomes both compass and chisel in the 4-S process:

- In **Self-Discovery**, it helps you trace inherited maps and misplaced meaning.
- In **Self-Development**, it shapes the path forward with tuned intentionality.

- In **Self-Mastery**, it aligns your response with deep resonance.
- In **Self-Knowledge**, it crystallizes inner coherence.

When lost in the depth of depression, the process of Self-Discovery felt overwhelming and chaotic. But eventually, the six Wh-Words gave me a foothold. They helped separate thoughts from emotions, sensations from beliefs, and illusory stories from grounded ones. Most of all, I began noticing how crucial it was to disentangle *intent from interpretation*—and *words from the identities covertly formed around them.*

Unlocking Perspectives: The Power of the Six Wh-Words

The six Wh-Words (what, why, when, how, where, and who) help you see how you have been shaping—and distorting—your own experience. The goal in this chapter is to use words with literal precision to deconstruct identity-based stories we habitually tell. Breaking apart the *what*, *how*, *when*, *where*, and *why* from the *who* brings amazing clarity. They help empty space from confusion with more honest questions seeking true clarity. They are cognitive coordinates that orient us. Here is a breakdown of their literal function:

What: Identity, Object, or Nature

What identifies, names, or defines something. The focus is on content. It doesn't ask how it works, why it exists, where it is, or who is involved—just *what* it is.

Why: Reason, Cause, or Motivation

Why seeks to understand motivation or cause. The focus is on causality. It doesn't describe the event, time, place, method, or who—but *why* it happened. *Why* is not intent, which carries direction and will. The distinction matters: *why* explains, intent directs.

When: Time or Sequence

When identifies the moment or period something occurs. The focus is on timing. It doesn't describe the event, reason, method, place, or who—only *when* it happens.

Where: Location or Context

Where asks about a physical or conceptual place. The focus is on location. It isn't concerned with what, why, when, how, or who—it's about *where* it occurs.

How: Method, Process, or Manner

How reveals the way something is done or happens. The focus is on the manner or mechanism. It investigates the means of action or experience, not what, why, when, where, or who—just *how* it works or operates.

Who – Person or Agent Involved

Who identifies a person or conscious actor. The focus is on identifying a being. Unlike *what*, which can refer to things or ideas, *who* always refers to a conscious agent.

By engaging these six Wh-Words with awareness, we shift from being defined by our experience to becoming conscious architects of it. This clarity about the words that shape our reality naturally leads to the next fundamental inquiry: if our language is a tool of construction, then who, precisely, is the *I* at the center of it all? In the next chapter, we turn our attention to this foundational presence: **I Am**.

CHAPTER FOUR

I Am

There was once a flame, born into a hall of mirrors. Everywhere it turned, it saw reflections—some larger than life, some distorted, some fading. It began to believe that these reflections defined it. That to grow, it had to shine brighter than the others. To belong, it had to match their flicker and dance in ways already choreographed by the hall.

One day, after exhausting itself trying to burn the right way, the flame dimmed. Its reflections grew faint. In that stillness, it realized it had never truly seen itself, only its echoes. So, it stopped searching outward and drew its light inward. For the first time, it noticed something the mirrors could never show: its source. It was not the reflection that gave the flame meaning. It was the flame itself.

I didn't set out to write about freedom. I set out to stay present through survival. This book was conceptualized during a long and unrelenting depression. At first, I thought I was writing something to help others; in truth, I was writing to help myself. The pages became a form of therapy, a mirror filled with raw projections, childhood echoes, moments of pride, collapse, defiance, and the slow unlayering of what felt true. This book itself is the sixth attempt, nearly seven years later, with each iteration evolving as the process of self-discovery unraveled more of what had opaqued the core presence.

Through it all, an old friend has accompanied me: curiosity. It kept me within a fragile measure of sanity as I searched outward for answers. Yet, curiosity did more than point toward explanations; it led me into unexpected places that became mirrors, helping me glimpse parts of myself that had remained just out of view. It moved through the things I thought I needed but didn't and unearthed what I had long kept hidden.

Curiosity kept whispering: *There's more. Keep going.* It never let me forget that something within me still wanted to be found. This book wasn't written from certainty; it was written from a thread I refused to let go of. Curiosity didn't rescue me. It simply refused to abandon me. And because of that, I didn't abandon myself.

I Am isn't something you become; think of it as the very first ripple in the undifferentiated field of Pure Possibility as it crystallizes into your unique presence. Before there was a name, a story, or even a question, that underlying pulse—the witness to it all—was already here.

This chapter is offered as an invitation to return to the flame behind the mirrors, moving beyond philosophical debate to direct experience. It is a journey to sense the unshakeable *I* beneath every *what*, *why*, *when*, *how*, and *where*. In the pages that follow, we'll explore the many facets of *I Am* through six angles of perception—guided by the foundational Wh-Words—so you can sense its presence rather than merely define it: *What are you? Why are you? When are you? How are you? Where are you?* and finally, *Who: I Am*.

As you move through these explorations, bring with you curiosity: the kind that seeks what is true without demanding reaffirming answers. Because once you notice the flame itself, the mirrors lose their hold. That shift changes everything.

What Are You?

The question *What Are you?* seems simple, almost factual, as if it asks for a scientific classification or physical description. The easiest answer tends toward role or identity. *I'm a teacher. I'm a mother. I'm an entrepreneur.* You may also say, *I'm a good person, I'm a genius,* or *I'm a failure.* These aren't answers to *what* but to *who*—persona and identity. They're stories—sometimes affirming, sometimes wounding, sometimes inherited or memorized. Later we will explore more about the *who*, but for now, let's stick to the literal *what* as a tool for deconstruction.

The Question of Substance

What refers to structure, substance, and observable form. It's the question we ask of an object on a table, the material used for construction, or an unidentifiable object flying at night. So when asked *What Are you?* you may begin with the physical. The body raises its hand first to describe shape, chemistry, motion; what is visible in this physical plane. The answer might be: "I *am* organic matter." "I *am* a biological system; a sentient being evolved from single cells." "I *am* a mammal belonging to the human species."

Perhaps you would go further in your definition: "I *am* human." "I *am* a temporary configuration of energy." "I *am* a composition of form, emotion, mind, and consciousness." "I *am* physical, mental, and emotional traits." Or further: "I *am* a soul." "I *am* pure consciousness." "I *am* mind." "I *am* spiritual." Or even further: "I *am* a creation." "I *am* a design." "I *am* a hologram." These can lead to further complexity: causation, purpose, sacredness, identity, temporality, and attribution, implying that life is a test, a design, a coincidence, or a calling, and each one with its own range of implications: destiny and autonomy, designed and evolved, divine and mundane, perfection and imperfection, immortality and mortality, superiority and inferiority. Notice the "am" in every one of those answers. What you believe you are made of often shapes what you believe you're meant for. Although some or all may point to something true, they do not necessarily answer the fundamental *what* of your being. The literal answer to *What Are you?* remains your choice to believe and formulate. Let your imagination fly. But whichever choice you make influences how you embody your *I Am*.

What differentiates you from all other life forms—from a plant, to an insect, to a whale, to another human? What would differentiate you from life forms on other planets? What would differentiate you from divine, inter-dimensional or super beings? Try answering without resorting to identity or persona. The literal "what."

Pulling from *The Ship of Theseus* as a thought experiment in philosophy, just as a ship may have every piece of its wood replaced over time and still be called the same vessel, are you defined by your physical components, by your function, or by the narrative of your story? Our body, mind, and emotions regenerate, decay, and shift, yet the presence within remains. Throughout this book, the journey is the answer, not the destination.

From Being to Doing: A Practical Distinction

While it's powerful to know what you are on an essential level, a practical disentanglement emerges from observing what you are *doing*, then recognizing how language, schemas, and emotions help attach meaning to those actions. Clarity begins with precision, and precision begins by asking: "What am I actually doing right now, in literal, observable terms?" The key insight is that the literal "What are you doing?" lives in tangible behavior. It's not a belief or an emotion; it's an action reflecting the experience you've chosen. Simply put: stepping on an ant. The *what* is literally stepping or not stepping on it. All the stories before or after are no longer *what*, but *why*, *when*, *where*, *how*, or *who*.

By translating identity-based beliefs into literal actions, you recruit the *Feedback Loop* to recalibrate your entire experience. When we habitually confuse the meaning of *what we are* with our intentions or feelings, we build illusions. This becomes especially dangerous during emotional spirals ("I'm worthless" or "I don't deserve") or relationship breakdowns ("I'm stronger" or "I'm weaker"). Your *what* is not your productivity, your praise, your pain, or even your decisions and actions. But these do reflect who you may *think* you are. Clarity of *What Are You?* as intended arrives with literal language and simple honesty. This may seem overly simplistic, but that's the point. Clarity dismantles illusion.

Reflection Questions

Let's now return inward. Knowing what you're doing is often the first doorway to discovering how you frame what you are. Observation, when honest, becomes revelation.

Ask yourself:

- Who—or what—am I identifying with when I answer *What Are you?*
- Is my answer a state, a role, a pattern, or a belief?
- Is this *what* arising from habit, fear, memory, or intuition?
- Am I mistaking what I do or feel for *what* I am?

Let the question *What Are you?* become a mirror.

Why Are You?

If *What Are you?* seeks to define substance, then *Why Are you?* seeks to understand causality. This deceptively simple question can be one of the most difficult to hold, primarily because the question itself is often tangled in expectation, more so than the answers being elusive.

We ask *why* and expect a noble response. We seek a cause, a justification, or a mission. We want to know the reason for our being. Isn't the question *Why Are you?* often answered with, "To fulfill a purpose"? Even the most sincere answers can carry a hidden charge: "Because I'm meant to do something great," or "Because my life must matter." While these are worthy aspirations, it's useful to notice when *why* becomes a performance of value or a justification for existence. This allows us to reframe the hidden *why* stories in our internal dialogue. For example:

Common *Why* Narrative	Probable Belief Behind It	Awareness-Based Reframe
"I'm here to fulfill a mission."	"I only matter if I achieve."	"Why am I tying my value to an outcome?" "What if my existence alone is enough?"
"I am here to improve."	"I am not enough."	"Why is this result the sole proof of my worth?" What if learning itself is the purpose?

Common *Why* Narrative	Probable Belief Behind It	Awareness-Based Reframe
"I was chosen for this."	"I must justify my being."	"Can I live with depth without tying it to a role?" What if simply being is justification enough?

Noticing your hidden *why* is a Self-Discovery move—spotting the belief. Reframing it into open-ended inquiry is Self-Development—choosing a new lens for your intention. Practice this: close your eyes, place a hand over your heart, and silently ask, "Why am I here?" Notice the first "because..." that arises.

Purpose can be expansive when aligned with awareness, but it can also become a trap when used to validate identity. When someone says, "I have a purpose," they often mean, "My life has meaning because I fulfill a role," or "I am worthy because I am useful." This creates a fragile form of value tied to doing, not being. In asking *Why Are You?*, be aware that the need to justify your existence may come from the belief that your existence alone isn't enough.

Used from identity, the question *why* may often lead you in circles of over-analysis, confusing interpretations, or even self-blame. Used with awareness, however, *why* becomes a tool for orientation. It no longer looks for justifying stories or for blame; it looks for alignment. Regardless of attributions, clarity arises when you can distinguish the layers behind your questions. Then, the *why* begins with your knowledge of your intrinsic worth and freedom, your engagement with focused intent (immediate motivation), the power to choose, and the meaning (the story) you decide to assign.

These reflections don't eliminate meaning; they allow it, even making room for value without validation. Sometimes, the most direct path to clarity is to redirect a disempowering *why* question altogether. When answering the question *Why Are You?*, it may be as simple as "Because I can," then deciding what is appropriate and conducive to your conscious aspiration. Now, *why* can realign with awareness rather than being tied to a fixed identity.

> Why Are You? *isn't a mission statement—it's the pulse of your presence.*

You exist because you exist. Everything beyond that is a story: tell it if it liberates you. Consider releasing it if it defines you.

Reflection Questions
Ask these questions to return to alignment with your authentic presence.

- When I ask *why*, am I seeking clarity or trying to prove I belong?
- What happens if I don't have a defined *life purpose* right now—am I still enough?
- What story do I use to justify my being, and what shifts if I stop using it as a defense?
- What if meaning didn't need to be assigned, but simply lived?

We now move from *why* into *when*—to examine how you relate to time, rhythm, and emergence in the next section, *When Are You?*

When Are You?

Time is more than a measurement of events; it is a context for being. You may say you live in the present, but how often does your mind rehearse the past, anticipate the future, or loop through stories that no longer belong to this moment? *When* is more than the time on a clock; it is a dimension of awareness. And for many, it may become a limitation.

> When Are You? *isn't about chronology—it's about where your awareness dwells.*

You might live today as if it were still yesterday, reliving guilt, replaying old arguments, or holding onto moments that shaped you more than you realized. Or you may constantly chase a better tomorrow, striving and hoping that the next goal will finally bring peace, meaning, or enoughness. The question *When Are You?* asks more than where you stand in time. It asks: When does your awareness truly dwell?

Working as a minister for many years gave me the opportunity to meet many people, each carrying a unique relationship to time.

For many, their past and future were central to their experience of being "faithful." The messages they heard, and which I often delivered, revolved around two pillars: forgiveness and hope. Forgiveness was often tangled with guilt and regret from the past. Hope was projected into a promised future: a place of love, peace, and an ultimate release from suffering.

Beneath those ideals, a subtle tension. The unworthiness born from past mistakes and the impossible task of forgetting deep pain. For many, the present was treated as a waiting room: a corridor between two powerful time zones—a past of both glory and guilt, and a future of both promised redemption and feared judgment. Life became something to be achieved or endured in anticipation of a later reward, rather than something to be lived now. This framing often masked a powerful question: Can you be fully present today if your story is written only in what was or what will be?

To live in the present is often spoken of as a spiritual ideal, but it is less about perfection and more about being. When you dwell in the past, your identity often becomes entangled with memory: "I was hurt," "I was successful." These become definitions. When you live in the future, you risk becoming trapped: you may endlessly plan and project, become frozen by fear, or remain stuck in hopeful waiting instead of taking present action. But when you are fully in the present, the *I Am* is not filtered through *then* or *someday*. It is unconditioned and alive. This does not mean the past or future have no place. **Memories and visions matter, but they are not where your awareness is meant to live.** They are tools. Not homes.

Each moment you recognize where your attention has drifted and gently bring it back to the now, you are not just practicing mindfulness. You are recognizing your core presence. The way you speak reveals *when* you are. A statement like, "I used to be a happy person," is a past-based identity. "I hope one day I can be happy," is future-deferred fulfillment. But "This is who I am right now" is a declaration of present-moment awareness. When you change how you speak about time, you change how you relate to it. These shifts may seem small, but their impact is profound.

- You wake up and say, “Why wake up today?” The day hasn't started; you are living in a remembered past.
- You say, “I'll be happy when I get the job.” The present becomes a means to an end, and fulfillment is exiled to the future.
- You say, “I'm doing the best I can right now.” That statement aligns your identity with presence and makes space for grace.

To bring this into practice, you can reframe the common ways temporal focus is confused:

Confused Statement	Awareness-Based Reframe
“When I fix everything, I'll feel peace.”	“Peace is something I can access now.”
“I used to be better than this.”	“Who I am today is a shift in awareness, not a failure of who I was.”
“If I lose this I'll be unhappy.”	“My happiness is rooted in how I choose to meet life now.”
“This always happens to me.”	“What is happening right now is new; it only feels familiar.”
“It's too late for me to change.”	“Everything I experience is now, so it is not too late to choose differently.”

Reflection Questions

- When do you most often direct your attention—past, present, or future?
- What internal language pulls you away from the present moment?
- Is your sense of self shaped more by what was, what might be, or what is?
- Are there moments in your day when you use the present only as a bridge to a hoped-for future?
- What happens when you stop trying to relive the past or rush the future, and just breathe where you are?

If *When* reveals when your awareness dwells in time, then *How* reveals the quality of your presence within it. The next question isn't about chronology; it's about rhythm, regulation, and resonance.

How you move through life reflects what you're aligned with now. This leads us to our next exploration.

How Are You?

A flame does not *try* to be warm, nor does it perform the act of shining. Its *how* is the ceaseless, underlying process of combustion—the fundamental transmutation of fuel into light and heat. Its *how* is its nature in action, not a mood or a choice. In the same way, the question *How Are You?* invites us to look beneath our behaviors and moods to the fundamental process of our own being.

> *Your* how *is the engine of being that continues beneath every story.*

Of all the Wh-Words, *how* is the one we most easily confuse with the *why* of behavior or emotion. When asked, "How are you?" we respond with a status report: "I'm fine," "I'm confused," or "I'm sad." We describe the *quality* of our experience, not the *process*. In this deep inquiry, *How Are You?* indicates something more fundamental. It points not to what you *do*, the level of certainty you carry, or what label you choose for an emotion, but to **the underlying** process **by which you are**. It describes the raw mechanics of your own *being*—your *I Am*, your consciousness in operation.

For many years I encountered many passionate people who expressed with joy their "awakening," "connectedness," or their certainty of being "saved." Whether or not it is, and their future is secured as expected, the *now* is what always matters the most. One could say, "I'm awakened," "I'm spiritual," or "I'm faithful." One could list all of what I intend, or even procure ways to ensure it is noticed, but your *how* is in your footsteps; listening, sensing, intending, focusing, participating. It is the living, impersonal engine beneath the personal stories you tell about yourself.

This shifts the focus from judging the quality of a state of being to simply noticing the machinery of being itself. By observing this, you disentangle the *I Am* from the performance of living. The following reframes help illustrate this distinction:

Common Answer (A Description of Action/Feeling)	Fundamental Process (The Method of Being)
"I'm good"	"I diagnose and process information."
"I'm trying to remain positive"	"I regulate an internal emotional response."
"I'm a good person."	"I execute a chosen moral framework."
"I'm feeling anxious about the future."	"I generate predictive scenarios based on past data."

By seeing the *how* as a fundamental process, you are no longer defined by the success or failure of your outcomes. You are the one whose nature it is to perceive, process, regulate, and generate. This awareness is what separates being from simply reacting. The moment you notice the *how* beneath your feelings and actions, you disentangle being from performance.

Reflection Questions

- Beneath your current actions and feelings, what is the constant, underlying *process* of your being? Is it perceiving? Thinking? Feeling? All at once?
- Can you sense the *how* of your existence as a continuous unfolding, rather than a series of tasks to complete?
- How does your sense of self shift when you identify with the *process* of perceiving, rather than with *what* is being perceived?
- What happens when you stop judging how well you are doing something and simply notice the fundamental *how* of your own awareness in operation?

The how *of your life reveals the fundamental process of your being.*

But every process occurs from a certain position, a particular place in your inner or outer world. This brings us to our next exploration: the underlying coordinates of our experience. Before you ask the ultimate question of *Who*, it is useful to first understand *where* you are standing.

Where Are You?

A river learns to move around the mountain rather than forcing its way through. Its current fluctuates naturally as the flow finds its way. *Where* water moves reveals its wisdom: it adapts and flows without pause or justification, interacting with the environment as it discovers possibilities. Its power lies not in its force, but in its intrinsic nature to find the *where*. And as it does, it carries with it the constant possibility for new life, alternative paths, and the spark for others to add their own meaning to the *what*, *why*, *when*, and *how*.

In the same way, **your *where* reveals whether you're meeting life with force or with flow.** You might rush, resist, or overthink, but the precision of *how* allows you to align with the *where*. In that alignment, the path reveals itself.

Your *where* is more than geography; it is a relationship between self and experience, intent and attention, perception and viewpoint. The question *Where Are You?* asks for more than a location. It points toward presence, direction, and the degree of alignment between your attention and your action.

> *Your* where *is not a place on a map, but the position of your awareness within experience.*

During childhood and teenage years, attending school was a genuine struggle for me. Staying focused in class felt almost impossible—and most of the time, I simply wasn't there. Where was I? Elsewhere. In the realm of imagination. That pattern followed me into adulthood. Only when I began working on the structural models of the Flow of Existence, did I realize, without the unnecessary judgment, just how often, and how naturally, I slipped into those inner-outer worlds, and how those were also useful expressions of my creative faculties.

Whether you call it fantasy, daydreaming, or simply generating alternate realities, the *I Am* moving through the mind doesn't limit creativity to the physical plane. Emotions, memories, and imagination all open other worlds—other experiences and imagined outcomes that can feel as vivid as any lived physical moment.

Trying to suppress these impulses is as pointless as demanding a river explain its own course. The question to ask here isn't *Why?* or *How?*—it's *Where?* Where will you channel this creative energy?

In Part III, we'll explore how to honor this impulse, using it as a strength by consciously choosing when to let your mind wander and when to bring its power back to where it matters. For now, the invitation is simply to locate yourself within your own experience:

- **Physically:** Are you grounded or dissociated from your body? Is your body the only *where* of being?
- **Mentally:** Are your thoughts scattered, focused, or wandering? Where is your imagination taking you? Is your mind the only *where* of being?
- **Emotionally:** Are you open, guarded, or in a state of avoidance? Are your emotions stored somewhere *else*? Is your heart the only *where* of being?
- **Spiritually (Attention + Intention):** Where is your attention aimed? Is your intention aligned with your attention?

Each of these *wheres* offers a clue about the position you are participating from.

Reflection Questions

- Where is your attention most often anchored—in a physical space or in your inner world?
- When discomfort arises, where do you go inside?
- Where are you speaking from — a place of experience or a place of pure aspiration?
- Where are you when you feel most yourself? Where are you when you forget?

Understanding *where* you are—physically, mentally, emotionally, and where you direct attention and intention—gives you a grounded sense of your position in the landscape of your life.

We have now mapped the *what*, *why*, *when*, *how*, and *where* of our experience. This complete orientation prepares you for the final, most central inquiry: to turn your awareness from the landscape itself to the one who perceives it all. We are now ready to ask, *Who: I Am*.

Who: I Am

It was a rare and beautiful day, with clear skies stretching across the highest peak on the easternmost edge of the Andes. That late afternoon, after completing my duties, I found myself in a moment of stillness. There was no immediate threat. The platoon lieutenant and first sergeant were tucked away in their underground bunkers, and I could saunter freely across the narrow, tapered crest of the peak, a reduced area carved by nature at the top of a pointed mountain. Our platoon's broader mission was to guard the massive repeater antenna stationed there, a critical link for communication between the highlands and the valley far below.

To the east, a deep canyon cut through the terrain, flanked by another mountain range. To the west, the land opened into endless valleys, where light danced on a faraway water mirror, blurring horizon and sky into one majestic sweep of color. It was serene and breathtaking. Still, in that golden hour of sunset, there was a kind of calm I hadn't felt in a very long time, especially in contrast to the constant tension pulsing through the valleys and jungles below. While battles raged regularly down there, this place offered a strange kind of peace, suspended between intensity and stillness.

From above, it was difficult to fully grasp the scale, or the senselessness, of what was taking place down below. At that altitude, people disappeared from view. From such a distance, everything looked still, simpler, almost meaningless. I had already struggled to understand how near-children on both sides were killing each other over a war that seemed to serve only the interests of the power-hungry, the severely wounded, and the corrupt—those in positions of influence far removed from the bloodshed. Up there, it felt even harder to make sense of it all.

Of course, every side can find reasons to justify war, often built on constructed ideals or moral imperatives, such as preemptive self-defense, liberation from oppression, restoration of justice, or religious duty.

These justifications often mask deeper motives like power, control, resources, or revenge. But looking down from that mountaintop, what struck me most wasn't the logic of those beliefs. It was the contrast. How small and invisible we seemed, and yet, how vast the destruction we could cause.

The ancient people who live on another mountain range not far from that peak call us "Younger Brother," a reference not to our age, but to our foolishness. It would take another twenty-four years before I had the privilege of sharing time with them and began to understand what they had seen clearly for centuries. They are as small as we are in body, yet in awareness, they are vast. They recognize how easily we act from unchecked impulses and from stories we've accepted without discernment—stories that fuel emotions we barely understand. We can climb high, not only on mountains but to a higher perspective, and look down at our lives from a place of serenity and clarity. Even when battling in the depths of our own internal valleys, we can rise above for a moment and see ourselves differently. This view contributes to insight of why, when, where, how, or who we are fighting, and what is worth seeing and choosing again from a higher perspective. From that kind of clarity, the path below can mirror the peace above.

From that mountaintop moment, one thing became clear: there is the *you* who observes. Not the identity that performs, proves, or protects. Not a one who asks *what*, *why*, *when*, *where*, or *how* from confusion. But the unconditional one behind it all. That is the beginning of the *Who: I Am*.

Many spend much of their lives answering *Who am I?* with scripted answers. We may confuse the *I Am* with the identities we've been assigned or constructed: "I am a provider," "I am successful," "I am broken," "I am a survivor." These are roles, personas, identities, and stories. While they may hold fragments of truth, they are not the source of it. If you say, "I am an architect," which voice is that? The profession, the story you're telling, or the unchanging *you* that holds both? If you change professions, are you someone else?

The *I Am* isn't a fixed label or feeling—it's the ever-present chooser, aware of its own existence; the one who feels, sees, and gives. It precedes every word you speak and remains free of every role and mood. **Before any label arises, there's the naked** Who: I Am: **pure presence, unbound and pregnant with limitless possibility.** This presence isn't conditional; it responds wherever your attention and intention flow. The more you rest in that unshakable *I Am*, the less sway those noisy identities hold—and the more your lived experience resonates with clarity and coherence. Like light filtered through clean or smudged lenses—or a symphony played on tuned or detuned instruments. The clarity of what emerges depends on your tuning. Whatever plays, it springs from your *I Am*.

This table helps distinguish between identity claims and identity awareness by reframing common *Who* statements, separating roles and conditions from the *I Am* that observes them.

Identity-Based Statement	Experience-Based Reframe	Insight
"I am a failure."	"I experienced a result I didn't expect."	Failure is an event, not who you are.
"I am the problem."	"I am experiencing an unresolved conflict."	Your being is not a problem.
"I am depressed."	"I am experiencing symptoms of depression."	You are not the label, but the one having the experience.
"I am broken."	"I am holding pain that hasn't yet met with understanding."	Your self is still whole, even when in pain.
"I am a [profession]"	"I chose this career and followed through."	A title, status, or position does not define who you are.
"I am a success."	"I've had outcomes that align with my goals and values."	Success is not who you are—it's a reflection of conditions and achievements.
"I am spiritual."	"I resonate with practices and beliefs that connect me to something greater."	These are ways of being beyond your essence.

Reflection Questions

Sit quietly. Let the roles drop for a moment. Ask:

- Who is observing this thought?
- Who is aware of this emotion?

- Who is present in this moment?
- Who is listening to an inner dialogue?

Don't answer too quickly. Let the question do its work. Notice what remains when all answers fall away. It is the *I* behind the what, why, when, where, and how. **That is you**, the source from which the core presence emerges, the source from which all experience originates. That is the one who is always free, always worthy, and always unconditional.

By now, you've encountered the six Wh-Words not as grammar tools, but as perceptual keys. They are how you locate yourself in presence (who), space (where), time (when), action (how), and causality and meaning (why). Each can serve as a lens of clarity or a layer of illusion. You are not the answers to these questions; you are the one who holds the capacity to ask them wisely. The *I Am* is the still center behind them all.

> *You are not the answers to what, why, when, where, or how—you are the one who asks and observes.*

This journey of awareness is not just about what you say or how you identify, but also how you relate to experience. And that brings us to our next foundation, where we explore how experience is shaped by contrast: the living dance of duality and polarity.

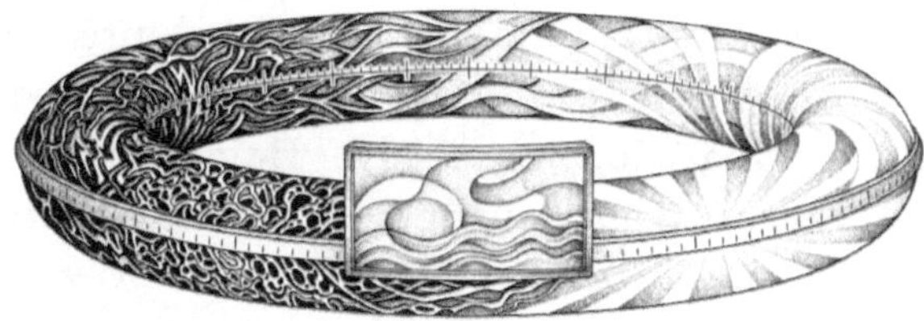

CHAPTER FIVE

Duality and Polarity

There are moments in life when experience feels split down the middle—right or wrong, good or bad, true or untrue. These distinctions seem absolute. But look closer. What appears separate may simply be two ends of the same thread: heat and cold, silence and sound, light and dark. We can be fooled not by the contrast itself, but by the belief that only one side can be true or right.

Awareness expands perception, revealing that you are not bound to either extreme but can move between them. Duality presents poles; polarity reveals the degrees between them. Freedom lives in your choice of how to engage with both.

Duality: The First Recognition

Before we can sense the subtle shades of experience, we meet life through contrast. The cold after warmth; the *no* after every *yes*. These distinctions awaken us to perception itself. Duality serves as a mirror, inviting us to see that two conflicting experiences can exist. In that moment of contrast, we become aware of choice.

I was seven or eight, waist-deep in churning lake water, trying to hold a boat steady against the pull of a storm. The wind whipped across the shoreline as the boat lunged with each wave. My father had backed the truck down the ramp, and I was doing everything I could to keep the vessel aligned—my arms shaking, my balance unsteady. I wanted to cry.

He saw my struggle and came around, frustrated and intense. I remember the look in his eyes and the way he locked in on mine: "Why are you going to cry? What's it going to solve? Hold the boat!"

That moment felt brutal, but it also taught me something. There was no apparent exit, no rescue. There were only two ways forward: I could feel sorry for myself and collapse under the weight of what I couldn't control, or I could hold the boat. Make the best of what was happening. That was a real encounter with duality as visceral awareness: two paths, one choice. I took the one of agency because it was mine to make, and it offered a path through the storm.

Duality shows up across all dimensions of life, presenting poles that help us distinguish our experience. Here are some examples:

- **Emotionally (Feeling Field):** Joy and Sorrow; Pride and Shame.
- **Mentally (Mindset Lens):** Clarity and Confusion; Focus and Distraction.
- **Physically (Bodily Spectrum):** Comfort and Pain; Movement and Stillness.
- **Spiritually (Meaning Axis):** Profound and Trivial. This is a polarity of significance.
- **Socially (Belonging Continuum):** Us and Them; Belonging and Exclusion.
- **Morally (Value Polarity):** Good and Evil; Innocent and Guilty.

In each case, there isn't a *better self* at one end and a *worse self* at the other. They're simply two sides of the same *field* (emotion, thought, body, etc.), and you're already inhabiting every pole in distinct moments. Your choice is where and how you lean into that field, shaping the quality of your experience. There is no *more* or *less* of you; your essence simply is, and all potential remains intrinsic. Whether you think of yourself as having minimal or infinite potential, the polarity at play is still potential. Where, why, when, and how you position yourself on that spectrum shapes the tone of your experiences. You always have a choice of which direction to lean, even as the fundamental potential you are navigating remains unchanged by your perspective. When duality is unexamined, it can become a cage.

- We may resist experiences that don't *fit* our label.
- We may vilify one half of a polarity to feel safe in the other.
- We may lose autonomy in our self-expression.
- We may react instead of responding with awareness.
- We may search for the *right side* rather than asking better questions.

Duality is not a restraint; it is the threshold where perception sharpens. But when we confuse a label with the truth, it locks experience into rigid binaries. Awareness allows us to see the space between the poles as a field of richness and movement.

Polarity: The Freedom to Move

A composer sits at the piano, exploring melodies, chords, and harmonies. Each note played is neither inherently right nor wrong, but positioned somewhere on a spectrum of consonance and dissonance, tension and release. The musician doesn't reject discordant notes as failures; instead, they offer contrast and texture, guiding the composition toward moments of clarity and beauty. You find the art of music not by eliminating dissonance, but by understanding its role in creating balance and movement. Just as polarity isn't opposition but relation, music is an interplay of tones that invites the composer to navigate gracefully through varying degrees of sound, ultimately crafting harmony from the entire range of expression.

There was a season when everything in me split into opposites: worthy or worthless, saved or damned. In the depths of depression, I could only see through the lens of duality. When the pain became too loud, and without knowing which questions to ask, I sought help, while employing an emotional and oxymoronized *assumption with certainty* that this would be the final attempt to find answers. It wasn't just through short-lived therapies and ceremonial sessions, but across philosophies, spiritual traditions, and scientific inquiries.

One concept I discovered made such a difference. It came from the book *The Kybalion* by the Three Initiates, and a principle that struck deep was Polarity:

> *"Everything is dual; everything has poles; everything has its pair of opposites; like and unlike are the same; opposites are identical in nature, but different in degree; extremes meet; all truths are but half-truths; all paradoxes may be reconciled."*
>
> — *The Kybalion*[2]

It was like a cold splash of liquid awareness. What if what I called failure wasn't the opposite of success, but simply a different degree of outcome, result, or achievement? What if the choice wasn't just between sadness and happiness, but a movement through different degrees of emotion? What if those degrees were swayed by wounds and unmet needs? What if even light and darkness were not opposites—but orientation within a spectrum of physical illumination? This wasn't abstraction. It was a relief. I didn't have to leap from one pole to the other as I mercilessly defined who I was or had become.

This principle is profoundly practical, and it rests on three recognitions:

1. **All Experience Exists on a Continuum:** Hot and cold are not different substances; they are varying intensities of the same energy.
2. **Opposites Are Identical in Nature, Different in Degree:** Qualities we see as contradictory are made of the same

2 Three Initiates, *The Kybalion: A Study of the Hermetic Philosophy of Ancient Egypt and Greece* (Chicago: Yogi Publication Society, 1908), 128

essence, just expressed differently. Like and dislike, clarity and confusion, confidence and insecurity.

3. **All Paradoxes Can Be Reconciled:** What seems to contradict at one level of perception becomes unified at another.

Duality divides experience. Polarity reveals where we are within it. Duality asks: *Which side are you on?* Polarity asks: *Where are you now, and which way are you moving?*

The spectrum from fear to courage is a primary example. Courage is found in the willingness to remain present with fear long enough to see a wider possibility. You don't need to leap from fear to fearlessness; you need only to shift from degree to degree.

In Fear...	Shifting Toward Courage...
"I can't handle this."	"I'm not sure yet, but I'm willing to begin."
"What if I fail?"	"What I learn from this will shape me."
"I need certainty before I move."	"Clarity can emerge through action."

This same principle applies to all polarities. The goal is not to eliminate one side, but to gain the freedom to move consciously along the continuum.

Exploring Other Spectrums of Experience

Here are further examples showing how this movement works across our channels of experience.

- **Body (Physical):** Overwhelm to Groundedness
  "I can't keep up" becomes, "I can pause, breathe, and feel steady in my body."
- **Mind (Cognitive):** Confusion to Clarity
  "Nothing makes sense" becomes, "I can begin by focusing on what I do know."
- **Heart (Emotional):** Loneliness to Connection
  "I feel I don't belong" becomes, "One honest moment can bridge me to someone else."

- **Spirit—Intention:** Drifting to Aligned Direction
  "I don't know where I'm going" becomes, "I can choose my next step towards clarity."
- **Spirit—Attention:** Scattered to Focused Presence
  "My mind is everywhere" becomes, "I can bring my attention to this moment."

The spectrum of self-worth is another fundamental polarity. Self-rejection says: "If I don't meet this standard, I am unworthy." Self-recognition says: "Even as I grow, I remain whole." One withdraws value; the other reclaims it. Worthiness is not a reward; it is your original state.

- "I need to prove I'm worth loving." shifts to "I love myself without needing proof."
- "They didn't choose me—what's wrong with me?" shifts to "Their choice doesn't define my worth."
- "If I fail, I'll be exposed as a fraud." shifts to "Even in failure, I remain whole."

Between silence and sound, there is tone. Between stillness and movement, there is rhythm. Between fear and courage, there is trust. Polarity is not a fracture— it is a spectrum of experience, an invitation to feel your way across the range with no need to choose either extreme. We don't exclusively live at the poles. We live through spectrums, where each moment is a shift in hue.

Duality gives us contrast; polarity gives us movement. Awareness allows us to notice both and move freely and consciously.

We've seen how duality and polarity shape the way we navigate life. But what happens before those polarities are even named? If polarity is the rhythm between the poles, perception is the lens through which we witness the dance. It contextualizes our experience and influences our beliefs. In the next chapter, we'll explore how perception, viewpoint, and perspective form the very scaffolding of our inner world.

CHAPTER SIX

Framing Your Reality

Perception, Viewpoint, and Perspective

You've now seen how experience, identity, and even emotional range can be tweaked by the energetic interplay of duality and polarity. Yet an even deeper dynamic continually recalibrates the path you walk: not just an event itself, but the lens through which you interpret and register it. That lens comprises three interwoven functions: *Perception, Viewpoint, and Perspective*. Together, these active architects of your reality determine what you sense, notice, how you interpret it, and where you believe yourself to be in relation to it.

This is where the model begins. Its central premise is simple: *Perception is reality—until awareness expands it*. Frames are workable once they're visible. We frame experiences. In doing so, we can easily confuse opinion with fact, reaction with stimulus, effect with cause, inherited belief with proof, and loose narrative with truth. Your perception may become your *reality*. This exploration reveals how your framing has room for expansion, and that by widening your lens you don't change who you are, you expand awareness, possibility, and probability.

The Anatomy of a Frame: Perception, Viewpoint, and Perspective

Seeing the world is not the same as knowing it. We rarely meet ourselves directly; more often, we meet the *frame* through which we're seeing. Let's briefly define the three functions of the lens that create it:

Perception

Perception is your experienced *reality*: the immediate, pre-conceptual registration of exteroceptive and interoceptive signals, with a first affective coloring before conscious concepts arise. It happens automatically—perception weights and tags signals for urgency/safety; it has not yet formed a narrative. A flash of bright green in your peripheral vision makes your heart flutter long before you identify it as "just a leaf." *Key idea: Perception is how you feel the world as real—whether or not it is objectively so.*

Viewpoint

Viewpoint is the positional angle or stance—literal and metaphorical—from which you look. It determines what enters the frame and what is occluded, and it sets salience by orienting attention (what's foreground vs. background). Change the angle, and the same event yields different data. Viewpoint selects the field of view; it does not yet explain or justify it. *Key idea: Viewpoint selects your field of view; it decides what enters awareness at all and what feels important.*

Perspective

Perspective is the interpretive story you create to make sense of what your viewpoint delivers; it explains and justifies. Shaped by roles, beliefs, culture, history, and values, it appraises and prioritizes meaning. You can hold multiple perspectives, widen a narrow one, or discard one entirely. This is where you remember that meaning isn't fixed; it's chosen. *Key idea: Perspective is the story you tell about what you see—and the one you can retell.*

Frames in Action: Five Stories

My former work in ministry, combined with years of observation, personal inquiry, and many interviews and conversations with people from many walks of life, showed me something deeper than the words they spoke: how we frame ourselves and others, often without even trying. From the extremely wealthy to those living in extreme poverty, from the self-righteous to condemned criminals, from puritan pious to sex workers, from the very young to the very old, and even with those who once fought on the opposite side of a senseless war; it wasn't just what people said, but where they were speaking from. I was a listener, an inquirer, but mostly, I was witnessing the way perception, viewpoint, and perspective shape our lived experience. Here are a few examples:

Example 1: "I'm not lazy; they are."
—Privilege offers one lens where effort is misframed.
A matriarch in a wealthy family expressed dismay at the "less fortunate" people she worshipped with, wondering aloud why they didn't simply work harder to escape their struggles (even if they were working two or three jobs to make ends meet).

- **Perception:** She noticed visible differences in lifestyle/effort cues.
- **Viewpoint:** From her position of privilege, she assumed the same doors of opportunity open equally to all.
- **Perspective:** Poverty looked like laziness or a lack of discipline, because she had never seen otherwise.

Her viewpoint filtered out the complexity of systemic barriers, framing poverty as a moral failing. This preserved her worldview but closed the door to a more empathetic, relational truth. Judgment presented as insight reinforced her frame.

Example 2: "Doors don't open for people like me"
—Scarcity tells a different story, where effort feels futile.
A young man grew up hearing, "We don't have connections and opportunities." After multiple rejections, he stopped trying, repeating, "People like us don't get in."

- **Perception:** He noticed obstacles more than openings.
- **Viewpoint:** From scarcity and class-based fatalism, life looked like a competition with limited slots.
- **Perspective:** Opportunity is guarded; effort won't matter.

Scarcity primed him to notice limitation, from which he concluded: opportunity is absent. The frame protected him from risk but narrowed possibilities. A mentor offered a reframe; he shifted his language (*Words Do Matter*) from *no opportunities* to "I'm building options." Soon, someone reviewed his portfolio, referred him to a paid internship, and unseen doors opened. His old belief gave way to a new one: "I create opportunity." The external world hadn't changed—but *how* he engaged with it had.

Example 3: "Do you know who I am?"
—Entitlement reframes reality through status.
A very wealthy young man broke down. He saw the woman he adored leave a restaurant with someone else. He was devastated. "I can't believe she chose that guy," he said. "He drives a Mustang! She's too beautiful for him! Why not me?! Life is so unfair!" His pain didn't seem to be about her decision, but about what her decision said about him, his worth, his masculinity, and his status.

- **Perception:** He registered exclusion and rejection.
- **Viewpoint:** From status entitlement, the expectation was preferential treatment.
- **Perspective:** Personal worth is based on status. Any lack of recognition looked like disrespect and injustice.

Through entitlement, his perception spotlighted status over fairness. The frame preserved superiority but closed off reciprocity, positioning romance as a transaction based on status, romantic success as validation, and her free choice into a story of cosmic injustice against him. Awareness could shift perception from demand toward relationship.

Example 4: "Everyone is against me."
—Victimhood magnifies vigilance until every signal feels hostile.
A man lived in a loop of pain. To him, the world was cruel, and people were selfish. Any suggestion to improve his mood was dismissed as "toxic positivity." He longed for confirmation more than new perspectives.

- **Perception:** From accumulated hurt, he scans faces, tones, and gestures for threat.
- **Viewpoint:** From victimhood and a fixed identity of the mistreated self.
- **Perspective:** Neutral or random signals seemed like deliberate attacks.

Vigilance heightened his perception, biasing what he noticed. Longing for confirmation more than truth, he framed neutral signals as threats. The frame confirmed the standing story ("everyone is against me"), filtering out disconfirming signals and reinforcing isolation.

Example 5: "Forgiveness meant letting them win."
—Forgiveness reframes conflict not as defeat but as release.
A woman spoke of a deep wound she had carried for years. When she talked about it, her eyes no longer flashed with resentment. They softened. "I forgave them," she said. "I was tired of the story owning me."

- **Perception:** She registered betrayal and hurt.
- **Viewpoint:** From resentment, forgiveness looked like giving up justice.
- **Perspective:** Anger felt safer than release.

Her viewpoint tied forgiveness to injustice, preserving anger as protection. This blocked release and kept energy bound to harm. In her story, we see a conscious reframing. The woman actively shifted her *Viewpoint* from the past event to her present well-being. This allowed her *Perception* to no longer be dominated by bitterness and anger. The result is a *new Perspective*—one where her own inner freedom is more valuable than being *right*. She reclaimed her authorship, choosing a story that serves her peace rather than one that keeps her tethered to a past hurt. She doesn't equate forgiveness with reconciliation or forgetting, setting her own boundaries. Awareness here could shift forgiveness into flow rather than concession.

Flow of Existence Slow-Motion Trace

Frames shape not only major stories but also ordinary moments.

Trace 1: 30 Seconds in a Hallway

- **Perception:** It begins with raw input. You hear the words, "You seemed quiet today." Your body registers a slight jolt; your mind parses the tone; your heart feels a mild sting.
- **Viewpoint:** You observe this from a specific angle—perhaps looking up from a position of feeling "less (or more) than" or sensing a power dynamic.
- **Perspective (Stage 5):** From this stance, your mind may draft two potential stories. One suggests, "I disappointed them." The other suggests, "They are simply checking in."
- **Attention (Stage 5):** This is the pivot point. Your focus collapses the possibilities, selecting one story to believe.
- **Manifestation (Stage 6):** The experience takes form. Depending on where your attention landed, you either withdraw in silence or engage with a clarifying question.
- **Feedback (Stage 7):** The moment ends, but the data remains. You notice the lingering tension or relief, signaling which Faculty—perhaps Worthiness (to unhook approval) or Will and Wisdom (to ask a clarifying question)—need tuning before the next loop.

Trace 2: The Crosswalk Snapshot

- **Perception:** A horn blares. Your body startles instantly, and your head snaps to the left.
- **Viewpoint:** You are standing at the curb, aware that you are in the driver's blind spot.
- **Perspective (Stage 5):** In that split second, two interpretations emerge. One frames the driver as

"aggressive," triggering resentment. The other frames the horn as a "warning signal," triggering caution.

- **Attention (Stage 5):** You choose which signal to amplify. Your focus locks onto one interpretation, effectively editing the reality you are about to live.
- **Manifestation (Stage 6):** Potential becomes action. You either freeze in anger or step back with a thankful nod.
- **Feedback (Stage 7):** As your heart rate settles, the experience informs your next step—reinforcing a belief or reminding you to stay alert.

Perception is not passive; it's a creative act. When we confuse our frame with the whole truth, we narrow possibilities.

"You don't see the world as it is. You see it as you are."[3]

Perception, *Viewpoint*, and *Perspective* define how we frame our reality—until awareness offers another way.

Once we begin to recognize how easily perception is shaped, and how deeply identity can be constructed around those perceptions, we naturally face a larger inquiry: If what I perceive is only part of the picture, and if what I believe about myself or others might be incomplete, then what is really *true*? And beyond that, what is *truth*? This next section invites a careful distinction between what is true from a viewpoint and what remains true regardless of viewpoint.

True vs Truth

In exploring the distinction between what is *true* and what is *truth*, we confront one of the most fundamental limitations of awareness: the limitation of *viewpoint* and *perspective*. Our minds are meaning-makers, our bodies are recorders of sensation, and our emotions are internal weather systems. Each channel of experience colors our understanding. What we call *true* is often only what is visible from where we are standing.

Imagine a cylinder placed in a room. Shine a light on its circular end, and its shadow falls on the wall as a perfect circle. Shine a

3 Anaïs Nin, *Seduction of the Minotaur* (Chicago: Swallow Press, 1961), 124.

light from its long side, and the shadow becomes a rectangle. Both shadows are *true* representations from their specific angles. But neither reveals the full shape. Only when you walk around the object, shifting your viewpoint and integrating multiple angles, does the *truth* of the cylinder emerge.

Everything we hold as *true* has been shaped by the angle we've lived from, the emotions we associate with our story, and the beliefs we've absorbed. What feels true may be emotionally charged but logically flawed. What is true in your experience may feel false to another because their vantage point, wounds, and wiring differ.

Why does this distinction matter so much? Because without it, we mistake our viewpoint for fact. Recognizing the gap between our *subjective truths* and the holistic *Truth* cautions against the arrogant claim of possessing absolute truth, for no single viewpoint can capture every angle. When we forget this, we don't just distort truth—we can weaponize it. Every extremist believes they are holding the whole or absolute truth. What they may hold is a single *true* piece, gripped so tightly that it becomes dangerous. In essence, while each perspective captures a fragment of truth, the larger truth is discernible only when all viewpoints are merged into one unified vision—making any claim of possessing the entirety from a single, limited viewpoint a fragile illusion.

When you realize that your version of the truth is a partial lens, a shift occurs. Certainty softens, and curiosity reawakens. You begin to ask: "What is missing from this view?" "What might be true from another angle?" "How can I hold my truth lightly, while still honoring what feels real to me?" This doesn't mean truth is relative. It means truth is *relational*. It reveals itself more fully the more perspectives you are willing to include.

Consider a simple example: a friend fails to call you back when they promised. You feel neglected. The *truth* of your experience may be: "They don't care about me." That is your *true*, from the angle of your hurt. But their *true* may be: "I've been completely overwhelmed and ashamed to admit it." Two partial *trues*, both valid from their own viewpoint. The relational *truth* is larger: there is distance in the connection, shaped by unspoken needs and mismatched assumptions. Awareness doesn't ask you to invalidate your truth; it simply asks: *What else might be true, too?*

> *Every true is a window. But no window shows the entire landscape. Truth is not an argument to win. It's a horizon to walk toward—together.*

If what I perceive is only part of the picture, what happens when we speak something that *isn't* true at all? This brings us to a revealing point of reflection: *A Lie is a Lie*.

A Lie is a Lie: True or Untrue

Once we realize that even our deepest-held beliefs can be shaped by angle, language, or emotion, we come to a harder realization: we don't just see partial truths—we also *speak* them. Sometimes unknowingly, sometimes with conviction, and sometimes even with good intentions. But what we say, and why we say it, still shapes our reality. Unlike the difference between *true* and *truth*, which depends on viewpoint, the distinction between true and untrue is factual. A lie remains a lie, regardless of the frame. This brings us to another revealing point of reflection: What happens when we speak something that isn't true?

> *A lie can be dressed in humor, hidden in tradition, or wrapped in kindness. But untrue is still untrue—no matter the costume.*

We often think of lying as a deliberate effort to deceive, but in the world of perception and perspective, it isn't always that clean. We lie to protect others, to avoid conflict, or because we're scared to be seen. Sometimes, a version of the truth feels too costly. And sometimes, we lie without knowing it—because we've inherited the lie, rehearsed it, or mistaken it for a worthwhile belief. This section approaches the topic through the lens of awareness, rather than morality or shame. Because if perception shapes experience, and language shapes perception, then the moment we distort truth, even subtly, we distort the foundation of our awareness.

Let me share another personal experience. I used to visit different venues to conduct sermons, and one day, as I was driving to one, a driver cut me off. "What an idiot! How dare she do that?" I reacted immediately, annoyed and angry. I quickly passed her, made the "do you think you are alone in the universe?!" face, cut very close in front of her, and kept going, grumbling under my breath.

As I pulled into the venue, I noticed she followed me in. It turned out she was attending the same sermon. I felt a wave of embarrassment. There I was, about to preach about love, compassion, and reconciliation, and I had just acted like anything but. That moment burned in my memory, not because I had a bad day or lost my temper, but because of what it revealed: Was I ashamed of how I acted, or just ashamed because I got caught? Would I have reflected at all if she hadn't walked through that same door? That's the thing about self-deception. It hides in plain sight. We think it's harmless, but it blinds us from within.

Let's be honest: it often seems easier or more comfortable to say what's untrue—to protect, to delay judgment, to keep the peace. The point isn't to shame ourselves, but to see what we're saying and why. Regardless of intent, a lie remains a lie: a statement that is untrue. This applies equally to the external messages we convey and to the internal narratives we tell ourselves, such as "I am unworthy" or "I can't." Recognizing this is essential for developing clear and honest awareness.

We don't always lie out of malice. Sometimes, untruths persist not because we intend them, but because certain cognitive patterns make distortion easier to sustain.

Cognitive Pattern	How It Can Support Untruth
Dunning-Kruger Effect	Overestimating knowledge, not realizing the claims are flawed.
Overconfidence Bias	Believing we are more accurate than we are.
Need for Cognitive Closure	Rushing to settle on an explanation, even if it's incorrect.
Confirmation Bias	Seeking information that validates what is already believed, ignoring what is true.

Cognitive Pattern	How It Can Support Untruth
Motivated Reasoning	Twist logic to reach an emotionally satisfying, but potentially untrue, conclusion.
Self-Serving Bias	Attributing successes to ourselves and blaming external factors for our failures.
Social Desirability Bias	Presenting ourselves in the best possible light, even if it's not entirely accurate.
Confabulation	Unintentionally fabricating memories to fill in gaps, believing them to be true.
Impression Management	Consciously shaping how others perceive us, even at the cost of truth.
Groupthink	Sacrificing truth for the sake of group harmony or consensus.

Such patterns remind us that awareness requires vigilance, not just good intent.

Sometimes, untruths are passed down without ill intent. A preacher shares a doctrine passed down from mentors, but years later, that doctrine is edited, replaced, or re-interpreted. Was the original sermon a lie? While not malicious, the statement *became* untrue, even if partially. A mother says Santa came down the chimney to leave gifts; the intention was joy, but the statement was false. If you say you were at the store but you were not, the statement is untrue. No shift in perspective makes it otherwise. Other times, the lie is revealed in the gap between our words and our actions, both external and internal. Someone says, "I care about justice and fairness," then they board a flight, ignore the 24 times the flight attendant asks to store small handbags under the seat in front of them, and cram all four carry-ons, including coats, backpack, and newly acquired merchandise, into the overhead bins, ignoring requests to leave space for others. They didn't intend to lie, but in that moment, comfort trumped fairness; the words weren't true in action. On an even subtler level, you might say, "I don't judge people," and then silently assign shame to a stranger walking past. No one else heard the lie—but you did. It happened in the inconsistency between your stated values and your inner reality.

Lying to yourself may feel harmless, but every time you do it, you reinforce the exact opposite of authenticity. You train your mind to tolerate distortion. You normalize dishonesty as a coping mechanism. Even white lies, when repeated, become the scaffolding of a false identity. They compound over time, forming a structure that feels stable but is built on sand. It binds you to roles you've outgrown. It dulls the sharpness of your awareness. It blurs the line between who you are and who you pretend to be.

Authenticity and self-awareness don't coexist with repeated, deliberate distortion. They require clarity, no matter how uncomfortable. Because when we confuse what is untrue with what is only partial, we lose the capacity to meet life honestly. Truth is not always easy, but it is always the path to inner freedom.

Once you notice the untruths you accept or repeat—especially the ones you tell yourself—you see how deeply they're tied to something else: the pressure to meet an invisible standard. A need to appear flawless, certain, or worthy. The illusion of the "perfect" self is one of the most persistent lies of all. But whose version of perfection are we comparing to, and what does it cost us?

Perfection as an Ideal

What is *imperfect* if there is no *perfect* to compare it to? We insist, "Nobody's perfect," yet that very admission dissolves the standard by which imperfect is defined. We label things as flawed everywhere, but flaws only emerge against an unseen ideal—an ideal we've never instantiated, exemplified, or even agreed upon. We use implicit, localized standards all the time—yet none amounts to a universal *perfect*. If no one alive ever met embodied perfection, then imperfection seems to have no anchor: it becomes a hollow label we tack onto ourselves and each other. Even the idea of perfection varies across cultures or traditions, making it even more unstable as a measuring stick. Why, then, do we chase a standard that cannot be found—to feel worthy, to avoid judgment—when the yardstick itself is merely an imagined mark in the air? What if perfection and imperfection alike are just constructs begging to be redefined?

The phrase "Nobody is perfect" sounds harmless, even reassuring. A phrase used to soften judgment, justify missteps, or to ground the one who implies they somehow are. But underneath it lies a subtle and corrosive construct. It implies that perfection exists as a flawless standard *somewhere* out there, and by that measure, we are always falling short. If every person is flawed, then the perfect human is either a myth or a contradiction. And yet, we build our lives—our religions, ideologies, and goals—around this idea, comparing ourselves to its image even as we say it can't be reached or clearly defined. It becomes an unreachable mirror: always present, never attainable.

This seed of unworthiness is deeply linked to the ideal of perfection because it creates a false condition for wholeness—suggesting we must earn what is already inherent. Somewhere along the way, you were taught—implicitly or explicitly—that you were not worthy, an idea born from beliefs that belonged to someone else. That joy must be earned. That love must be deserved. That mistakes require penance. That your value increases the closer you come to some imagined ideal. How silly does this sound: "You are perfect as you are, but nobody's perfect, so you can't be. Therefore, work hard to become a little less imperfect."

Perfection, then, seems designed not to be reached, but to keep you reaching, and imperfection seems designed to keep you as a clone of others' expectations. Neither invites you to be authentic. Both demand that you perform. Authenticity asks, "What is true for me right now?" Perfection replies, "What should I be to be enough for them?" One liberates. The other edits. The more you strive to appear worthy, the more you abandon the one thing that is already whole: your unfiltered being. You end up polishing a mask rather than expressing a self.

When perfection is framed as an unattainable moral or spiritual ideal, it sets the conditions for judgment. From decades in ministry, one of the most widespread teachings I encountered was this: "*No one is perfect. We are all sinners in need of grace.*" It sounds humble until you examine its undercurrent: *You are broken, therefore you must be saved. You are unworthy, therefore you must either prove your value or accept that you will never truly deserve.* This framing breeds dependence. It keeps you small while appearing to offer freedom, and it justifies judgment—not only of yourself but of others. If I'm flawed and trying, and you're flawed and failing, then I feel closer to the ideal. Guilt becomes the currency of belonging. Shame becomes the cost of deviation. Perfection becomes the judge that sits in every room.

What begins as an abstract ideal soon becomes relational currency. From this place, comparison becomes the bridge we build to measure ourselves. We may see others through the filter of projection, casting onto them the parts of ourselves we either reject or idolize. If someone appears more disciplined, more spiritual, or more successful, we may see who we think we should be. Likewise, when someone fails or shows vulnerability, we often see a mirror of what we fear in ourselves. Judgment, in this sense, is self-directed but disguised as observation.

We do this to validate our distance from failure or our proximity to worth. We project our inner standards onto others to protect ourselves from confronting our own sense of lack. In this way, perfectionism turns relationships into evaluations. True connection becomes difficult, if not impossible, when every encounter is a contest shaped by criteria that no one can fully meet—because the criteria themselves are illusions.

You are not perfect. You are not imperfect.
You are not a measurement.

You are the one who measures yourself—the one who observes the shifting criteria, questions the ideal, and reclaims the right to define alignment, not in comparison to others, but in coherence with yourself. Perfection, as it's often framed, can be deceiving. But awareness reveals that it is not a destination. It is a process: an evolving movement toward internal coherence, clarity, and integration. It is not the absence of difficulty, but the ability to see through it; not the erasure of what's misaligned, but the capacity to reorient without self-rejection.

I Am is already whole, already perfect in its essence. Your thoughts, words, and actions are not a measurement of your being, but a reflection of how aligned your expression is with that deeper realization. To seek perfection as an identity will inhibit you. To live as awareness, and to recognize alignment as the measure, invites you into *authenticity*. Consider perfection, then, not as a static state, but as the harmonization of apparent opposites into a living, adaptive balance: a dynamic process of reconfiguration and a subtle, ongoing attunement between your intentions and your experience.

Flaws appear when the measuring stick keeps shifting. But you are not the flaw. You exist to *be* authentic. Alignment evolves moment by moment, degree by degree. Let go of becoming perfect—or being imperfect. *Be.*

Reflection Questions:
Beyond the Mirror of Perfection

These are not answers to chase, but mirrors to look into. You don't need to respond; just notice what stirs.

- When did you first learn what *perfect* meant, and what shaped that definition?
- What do you believe would make you worthy of love, success, or peace?
- How often do you compare your current self to a version of yourself that doesn't exist?
- What aspects of yourself have you come to label as flaws, and when did they begin to feel that way?

Gratitude and the Solutionic Challenge Model

We've reframed the ideal of perfection and released the weight of unworthiness. But what do you do when life still feels difficult, when a situation is undeniably hard, when challenge presents itself in the real, living moments of your experience? This is where awareness shifts from observation to application, and gratitude becomes more than a feeling; it becomes a key.

What if this isn't a problem? What if this is the moment everything shifts?

A challenge is more than an obstacle; it is a configuration of perception, belief, energy, and potential. We can approach problems by asking, "How do I fix this?" But the proposed *Solutionic Challenge*

Model invites a deeper reframe: "What is this asking me to become aware of?" or "What new configuration wants to emerge from this tension?" Every challenge is a mirror, not of failure, but of evolution. It reflects where you are ripe for redirection.

What we call a "problem" is often the friction caused by an outdated configuration—a belief or perspective that no longer resonates. When that friction arises, it's a signal; an invitation. Gratitude is what opens the gate. Not forced gratitude, not spiritual bypassing, not toxic positivity. It is a conscious willingness to say: "I see the discomfort, and I choose to meet it with awareness." That act of choosing is itself an act of courage. It's a movement that whispers, "There's more than what fear is showing me." Gratitude subtly reshapes the challenge. It doesn't eliminate pain or discomfort, but instead shifts the frequency at which that experience is received. Your perspective expands, your attention refines, and what emerges is born of alignment. What once felt like a dead end may become a living threshold.

> *Gratitude is not a mood; it is the key that reframes a problem into a threshold.*

Engaging with a challenge *solutionically* follows a clear path:

1. **Awareness:** You notice the situational tension without labeling it by default as *wrong* or *bad*.
2. **Inquiry:** You ask not *why is this happening to me?* but *what is this trying to reveal through me?*
3. **Attunement:** You tune into what feels distorted and what feels aligned within you.
4. **Gratitude:** You hold space for the experience—even the difficult parts—as part of your conscious navigation.
5. **Choice:** You choose a response aligned with clarity, not a reaction born from habit.

Each step moves you from *problem* to *possibility*. This applies equally to setbacks and to successes that feel strangely empty.

Consider this first scenario: you didn't get what you wanted. The job fell through; the relationship changed. Your default response might be, "What's wrong with me?" "This is what I deserve," or "It's their fault!" Through a *solutionic* lens, the challenge is not your worth or that of another; it is how you're interpreting the experience. Instead, try asking: *"What is this challenge inviting me to become aware of?"* or *"What is being revealed or reconfigured?"* Sometimes, the disruption is the solution, because it interrupted what may never have been aligned.

Now consider this second scenario: you got exactly what you asked for. The deal closed, you reached the goal. On the outside, it looks like success, but internally, something is off. There's tension or exhaustion. This is a disguised challenge. Instead of thinking, "I should be happy, why am I not satisfied?" ask: "What part of me believed this would be enough?" or "What does this teach me about what I've outgrown?" Sometimes, getting what you want is the clearest way to see what you no longer need.

The purpose of gratitude here is to recognize that meaning can emerge even from the most difficult experiences. In your conscious experience, gratitude is what lets the light in, revealing that what you called a wall was actually a door in disguise. You don't need to like the challenge. You may meet it with the awareness that: *This, too, belongs*.

Reflection Prompt: From Problem to Possibility

Choose one recent situation that felt like a problem, whether it was a setback or a success that felt strangely empty. Then ask:

- What did I expect this experience to prove about me?
- Was this aligned with freedom and authenticity, or with fear and validation?
- What was the actual challenge beneath the surface event?
- What is the deeper invitation now available to me?

Let the answer emerge without blame or justification, but as awareness—your clearest compass.

Gratitude opens perspective. Reframing transforms attention. The ideal turning point comes when you no longer seek answers to fix every problem, but instead meet the moment with authentic presence. If the *Solutionic Challenge Model* helps you reinterpret difficulty, authenticity helps you respond from your center. Let us now explore what it means to live the *Power from Authenticity* as an expression of inner coherence.

Power *from* Authenticity

It was in the northern mountains of the Andes—where clouds drift like slow prayers over untamed valleys—that something essential loosened inside me. I hadn't gone searching for answers with scholarly intent; I went because something unnamed pulled me there. I needed to step away from the structures I'd spent years building.

We walked for many hours, tracing a long path up into the highlands, and I stayed mostly silent. One of the Mamos spoke often on subjects ranging from politics to prophecy, faith to football, each topic arriving and dissolving like a cloud. I listened without debating or resisting. Instead of my usual compulsion to control the narrative with questions or performance, I found something I didn't realize I was missing: stillness.

The journey was full of rhythm, texture, the sound of our feet against the earth, and the astonishing clarity of being somewhere that didn't need my voice or opinion. With every step, I was being unfastened from the habit of filtering experience through old roles. The mountains didn't care who I had been. The tribe didn't expect me to be anyone else. The moment required nothing but presence.

As we climbed, the silence spoke louder than any doctrine I'd preached. I noticed how often my inner world had been shaped by the illusion of control—how I'd once believed that to feel safe, I needed to know what would happen next. But here, in the *opportunity of not knowing*, something deeper emerged. And in that, a heaviness I didn't realize I'd been carrying—the weight of performing, pleasing, and knowing—began to dissolve, even if for a while.

It wasn't force that brought release. It wasn't achievement that opened the way. It was the unexpected simplicity of surrender—an inner permission to let presence take its rightful place. This wasn't a breakthrough I could frame with logic. It was a loosening in the body, a softening behind the eyes. Where I had once tried to command meaning into form, I now allowed the moment to shape me instead.

For the first time in years, I experienced a moment free of performance. No mask to adjust. No role to play. Just presence. Just breath. Just being. That walk wasn't a destination; it marked a threshold. You can cross it by loosening your grip, allowing what no longer serves to fall away and returning to what has always been there.

This is the power that comes from authenticity. It isn't a performance of uniqueness or a curated version of truth. Authenticity is the coherence between *I Am* and your outer expression; the alignment between your core presence and the way you live, speak, and move in the world. When you express from that place, choosing to participate rather than to impress or protect, you feel something unmistakable: *alignment*. Your *Body* grounds, your *Mind* clears, your *Heart* opens, and your *Spirit (your Attention + Intention)* flows effortlessly.

When you are aligned, there's less friction and second-guessing. Your actions arise from presence. This is evident across all your *Channels of Experience*:

Channel / Signal	**Aligned (Authentic)**	**Misaligned (Inauthentic)**
Body	Grounded posture, full breath	Tension, shallow breathing
Mind	Clear, supportive self-talk	Self-doubt, over-analysis
Heart	Open resonance, compassion	Numbness, reactive loops
Spirit	Choices flow from an inner "yes"	Guilt-driven obligation or avoidance

Living from authenticity is like clearing static from a signal. Your intentions land clearly, and your connections run deeper. This authenticity becomes its own kind of power: quiet yet compelling, simple yet transformative. It doesn't demand attention; it naturally draws it, revealing three ways you can express this power:

1. **Reclaim:** You direct from your *authentic self* without distortion.
2. **Discover:** You lean into insights that arise when external filters drop and curiosity takes the lead.
3. **Emerge:** You express something wholly original that is uniquely yours—an embodiment that comes only from *I Am*.

These are un-sequenced expressions of your intrinsic freedom and worthiness, and the endless possibilities you have access to. Authenticity is the thread woven through all that follows. It shows up in what you choose to believe, how you respond to feedback, and how you relate to your roles. You don't need to force it; you only need to notice when you're aligned and when you're not—and choose again. When you do, even probability multiplies.

Authenticity is not performance—it is the clear signal of your being, transmitted without distortion.

When you speak, move, and decide from that place of inner alignment—without masks or agenda—something shifts in the field around you. People lean in. Doors open. Opportunities you never imagined appear simply because your genuine presence carries an unmistakable magnetism.

Practices of Superconductive Authenticity

When you drop filters, dissolve distortion, and release limitation, authenticity becomes superconductive—like a current moving without resistance. The more aligned you are with your authentic signal, the more cleanly energy moves through your system—*Body, Mind, Heart,* and *Spirit (attention + intention)*. These practices help you stay attuned to that state where possibility accelerates and action harmonizes with presence.

Reclaim Possibility

- Bring attention to a decision you're currently holding back on—not out of discernment, but out of fear, doubt, or external pressure.

- What would this choice look like if you weren't trying to protect an image, avoid conflict, or gain approval?
- What would shift if you trusted your authentic signal more than the expected outcome?
- Try taking one action from that authentic current and observe the energetic effect.

Open the Circuit (Discover)

- "What am I filtering right now?" Let answers arise without effort. It may be something you're afraid to speak, a desire you've dimmed, or a version of yourself you're trying to manage.
- Now ask: "What if nothing had to be hidden?" Feel the difference in flow. Let that openness become the new standard for your presence.

Conduct the Signal (Emerge)

- Choose a moment in your day to move, speak, or create without agenda—no performance, no rehearsal. How does your body move when it's not trying to control perception?
- What words come when you're not editing for impact?
- What becomes possible when you trust the moment more than the outcome? Let the experience reflect what happens when energy moves without resistance.

Let that feeling of presence be your home. Return, again and again, to the place within you that never performs—only remembers how to be.

We began this chapter by exploring the frames that shape our reality—from perception and truth to the illusions of perfection and the power from authenticity. We now turn to the very substance that gives these frames their strength. Our frames are built from the energy of what we hold to be true. In the next chapter, we will examine the spectrum of this energy: *Belief, Faith, Conviction, and Knowledge*.

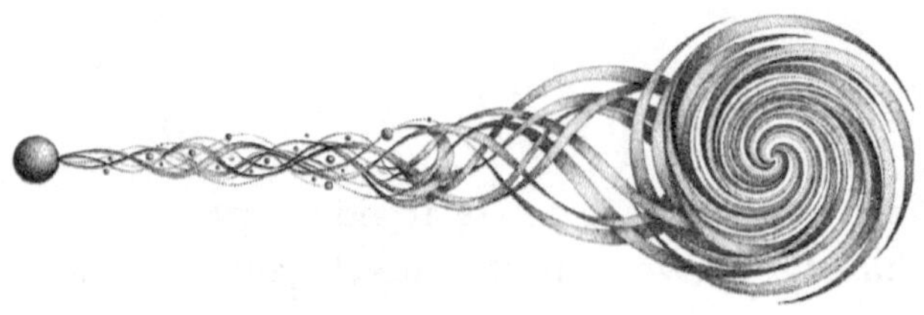

CHAPTER SEVEN

Belief, Faith, Conviction, and Knowledge

There are moments when the urge to teach gives way to the need to listen. And sometimes, it's in that pause—when you don't respond, defend, or correct—that real learning begins.

It was my first night in the diplomat's village, the ceremonial head of the four tribes who inhabit the region. After hours of climbing steep paths through the Sierra Nevada, we settled into a clay hut with a small group of Mamos and sat by firelight. I listened as one of them—calm, thoughtful, and unwavering—shared the long-held grievances of his people. He spoke of generations of outsiders who had come not to learn but to convert. Many had claimed to carry the truth, yet all contradicted one another. He told stories of children taken from their families for indoctrination, of ancient ways dismissed as evil, of accusations of witchcraft and warnings of damnation. One preacher after another, each with a different interpretation of a common scripture, was somehow sure that theirs was the only valid way.

He was not angry as he shared this; he was resolute. They weren't aware of my decades in ministry. I hadn't shared it because I had come to listen, not to teach or preach. Still, I recognized the irony. I had, in other chapters of my life, embodied the very certainty he was now challenging, and I knew that offering my own clarifications wouldn't change their past experiences.

As he recounted the patterns of judgment, something in me was stirring, like sediment in water newly unsettled. He hadn't confronted me, but I was witnessing something that didn't fit an inner structure I had built: a people who were more reverent, more peaceful, and more attuned to the essence of the teachings I once believed I understood than many who had claimed to live by them.

Throughout the time spent in that village, the silence between us became more instructive than any doctrine. Their respect for nature, their system of governance, their commitment to balance, and the depth of their lived wisdom; none of it aligned with the accusations they had endured. In fact, their way of life embodied many of the very values others had tried to enforce through conversion. I hadn't traveled there to convert or to compare. I had arrived, driven from cognitive and emotional dissonance, riddled by newly formed and unanswered questions; seeking clarity beyond the familiar noise I came from. What surprised me was not just the depth of their way of life, but how much I had misunderstood about *Belief*, *Faith*, *Conviction*, and *Knowledge* (*BFCK*).

At some point in life, we may find ourselves clinging to beliefs handed to us without deeply examining them. This was not just about religion; it was about perspective. I realized I had spent many years defending not just what I believed to be truth, but a preferred narrative of who I thought I was. Like many others, I had used the words belief, faith, conviction, and knowledge interchangeably, as if they all meant the same thing. They don't. Understanding the difference makes a profound difference.

For years I worked with youth groups and congregants from many countries. When their religious beliefs were questioned, they frequently asked, "What do we believe in?"—a question that essentially meant, "Tell me what I should believe." For many, young or old, *faith* is often about reaffirming an identity, regardless of evidence or personal experience.

To see how these concepts influence the way you meet life, it helps to first differentiate them:

- **Belief** is accepting something as true, with or without evidence, even if evidence is often obtainable. We often carry beliefs (religious or not) without realizing it until they are challenged. Beliefs tend to form through culture, upbringing, authority figures, or repeated exposure.
- **Faith**, in its traditional sense, involves trust in something without objective proof. If belief says, "I think this is true," faith says, "I trust this is true, even if I can't prove it." This kind of faith often arises in religious or existential contexts and is shaped by deeply held narratives. It represents a deeper alignment with the unknown—fueled not by certainty, but by commitment. When faith sustains alignment long enough to be tested and verified, it crystallizes into knowledge—lived recognition of what endures as true.
- **Conviction** is when belief hardens into identity. It may or may not be accurate, but it feels immovable, offering a sense of certainty—often at the cost of openness. Conviction can also harden belief into rigidity, but it can steady your stance when clarity demands courage.
- **Knowledge** refers to what is supported by empirical evidence, verification, or direct and verifiable experience, and is, ideally, falsifiable. It can evolve as new information emerges, but while we hold it, knowledge forms a foundation for interpretation and decision-making.

The fact that something is widely believed, deeply felt, repeatedly stated, or powerfully defended does not make it true. Millions believed the Earth was the center of the solar system; their belief didn't make the sun orbit Earth. Yet these four terms are often treated as interchangeable, especially when they support what is preferred. This matters not only in intellectual debates or theological discussions, but in everyday life. It shapes how you relate to people with different worldviews, how you interpret unfamiliar ideas, how you define what you consider real, and even everything about how you see yourself. A person who believes in angels may base that belief on tradition, anecdotal stories, or personal encounters. Another who believes in fairies may have similar grounds. True or untrue, one of these beliefs is often considered more valid than the other, not because it's more verifiable, but because more people share it. And that's the hidden hinge: social reinforcement is not the same as truth. When you start to see how loosely they can be applied, it opens the door to a more expansive awareness. Awareness of filters. Awareness of how conviction can masquerade as knowledge. Awareness of how you can dismiss others' beliefs without examining the grounds of your own. This chapter invites you to pause before declaring something true or false—not to promote doubt, but to promote depth. It encourages a kind of intellectual humility that allows for perspective without requiring agreement.

In practice, these concepts play an intimate, everyday role in constructing identity. We adopt internal frameworks to define who we are, and these frameworks influence our choices, shape our personas, and anchor our sense of self. Some of the strongest inner narratives are not grounded in knowledge, but in unexamined beliefs like, "I'm not worthy of love," "I'm not good enough," or "I'm morally superior."

We hold a kind of *faith* in our limitations—*faith* that "Nothing ever changes," "You can't trust anyone," or we use faith to justify patterns, as in: "Everything happens for a reason." Similarly, convictions about who we are can be just as binding. The statement "Good people always put others first" may sound virtuous, but it can lead to chronic self-neglect, burnout, and resentment.

This is where the *Verbal Architecture* we explored earlier becomes so important. Self-statements reflect and reinforce internal frameworks we've absorbed: "I can't..." (when we may mean "I won't" or "I don't want to"); "I have to..." (when we may mean "I choose to" or "I'm afraid not to"); "I am..." followed by traits that were assigned to us rather than chosen. Through language, you confirm what you believe, as an expression of your inner freedom, even if those beliefs do not serve your *authentic expression*.

This awareness is an invitation to observe: *What belief am I speaking from when I say this? What am I reinforcing with this conviction?* The more aware we become of the difference between these concepts, the more consciously we can align the facets of our being.

A Force of Alignment

This leads us to a deeper reframing of one of the most powerful forces. We will now explore what happens when you begin to see *faith* not as passive acceptance, or a qualification of a religious belief, but as an active energetic configuration: a *sustaining force* that strengthens presence, fuels courage, and directs creative momentum.

Consider *faith*, in this context, as more than belief. As a *force of alignment*, a generator of continuity and coherence that doesn't simply hope for the best, but shapes the conditions that allow transformation to occur. It is what carries you when you cannot yet see the outcome, but know you are aligned.

Faith as a sustaining force opens access to deeper potential and fuels possibility. To act from this kind of *faith* is not to trust blindly that things will happen; it is to participate in *how* possibilities emerge, guided by a deeper alignment than appearances alone. In this sense, *faith* focuses the field of possibility just enough to move from belief into manifested reality. This is not blind trust. It's active participation in possibility—an energetic coherence that sustains momentum.

BFCK and the other Foundations

The distinctions between BFCK influence how we perceive, decide, and express ourselves. To fully integrate their impact, it helps to revisit the foundational concepts of this book.

In Words Do Matter (Chapter 3): The way we speak reinforces what we believe. "I'm bad with money," "I can't be biased—I'm very objective," "My intuition is always right," or "I'm just not a 'math person'" may not be knowledge; it might be belief disguised as truth, repeated until it calcifies into conviction.

In I Am (Chapter 4): Our core awareness, *I Am*, exists before belief. But as we grow, we layer beliefs over that awareness: "I am not enough," "I have to earn love." These are not truths. They are constructs. Faith, reframed as a sustaining force, helps restore clarity.

In Duality and Polarity (Chapter 5): *Belief* often lives in duality: right vs. wrong, good vs. bad. Conviction can harden those polarities. Awareness expands when we allow belief to move along a spectrum, recognizing that: If *Belief* is a perspective (the lens you hold), *Conviction* is its intensity (how strong you hold it), and *Faith* is the energy that sustains exploration (the charge that propels you to explore beyond your current lens), then *Knowledge* is the coherent understanding that crystallizes when perspective (belief) and intensity (conviction) are tested and validated through faith-charged exploration.

In Perception, Viewpoint, and Perspective (Chapter 6): What we call "knowledge" is often an assembly of perceptions shaped by belief. But when we challenge perception and belief, new truths can emerge. *Conviction* becomes meaningful when we recognize it as a reflection of lived coherence, not just ideological certainty. *Belief* becomes an entry point, not a destination. Each one can either reinforce limitation or support liberation.

> *To live in expanded awareness means becoming conscious of what we believe, honest about what we don't know, courageous in what we hold by faith, and humble in what we claim to know.*

That is the terrain of Self-Discovery. That is the unconditioned expression of the *Authentic Self.*

Reflection Questions

- What do I believe to be true about myself, and where did that belief originate? Is it based on experience, repetition, someone else's voice, or something deeper?

- When have I held faith in something without evidence, and how did it shape my choices? Was it empowering or limiting? Did it open new possibilities or close them?
- Where has conviction helped me grow, and where has it held me back? Can I recall a time when certainty blocked my capacity to listen, learn, or evolve?
- Am I at liberty to change my mind about my self-perception and other beliefs? Am I still clinging to ideas that were never truly mine?

We've explored how *what we believe, hold by faith, cling to in conviction,* or *claim to know* all shape our internal world. But these beliefs don't exist in a vacuum. They express themselves *through* us—through the *Body*, the *Mind*, the *Heart*, and the *Spirit (attention + intention)*. In the next chapter, we will map those four channels of experience and how, through awareness, we can tune the inner architecture of the self.

CHAPTER EIGHT

Experience, the Dance of Life

The Beginning of the End, and Something Beyond

At 18, one year into a season of life marked by early ministry, I was drafted into a senseless war. My deployment lasted only eight months because in the eighth month, I was severely injured in combat.

We were ambushed. A mine exploded roadside, followed immediately by gunfire. Our truck—a civilian vehicle repurposed for supply transport—was destroyed. We followed protocol: disembark, flank, repel. But chaos ensued. I had sustained 24 impacts across my body, mostly shrapnel. Both lungs were punctured. Yet, remarkably, my body bore only scars and internal injuries that, compared to what might have been, felt survivable. Others received fewer impacts and were left in far worse condition.

We were teenagers in combat, trained yet unprepared for the depth of what we were about to endure. As bullets flew and choices collapsed into milliseconds, we each did what we could: fight, freeze, run, cover, help, survive. The complexity of that moment lives in every one of us—etched in emotion, memory, body, and the intent to survive it, then and through life. At first, I didn't know I'd been hit. I saw specks of blood on my arms but felt no pain, thinking it wasn't mine. Then the breathlessness came. I tried to load my weapon, but my arms were heavy. I couldn't do it. I turned to the soldier beside me. "Jimmy," I said, "load my gun." He looked at me, terrified, and shouted for help. I didn't understand until he screamed louder, begging others to come. He thought I was going to take my life to avoid being captured and tortured. "Just load my gun," I repeated. "No! What are you going to do?" he cried.

Another soldier appeared. He moved with precision. He carried a frozen soldier who sat in shock to safety. Then another, then me. All while the firefight raged on. No one died.

We were loaded onto another truck—five of us, headed somewhere, anywhere safer. I couldn't lie down; I couldn't breathe. I sat on the edge of the truck bed with my legs hanging, gasping in rapid-fire breaths to stay conscious. A soldier beside me kept checking on me. I felt like a wounded animal: alert, trembling, and dying. And then, I felt as if everything began to transform.

It wasn't physical or mental. It was something else. Reality shifted, as if fog had entered a room. Sound faded. Time slowed. I knew—*I knew*—I was dying. This came not as fear, but as a form of awareness, a clarity beyond thought. I felt it: *that place*. A field of endless peace, love, and serenity where everything made sense. I could feel God, Source, or the All—the *everything* that makes you stop needing to understand. And I knew if I let go, I could stay there. Then, I saw the faces of my family in a collage. The question arose: What about them? A response: They'll be okay. I surrendered.

But pain pulled me back, excruciating pain in my back. I tried again, but each time I attempted to lie down to cross over, I couldn't breathe. I looked back and saw myself lying there. Dead. Mouth open, eyes fixed. Gone. And then came something not as a voice or a thought, but as a directive: Stop trying. It is not your time. There is still more to do.

Was it my higher self? A guide? My sense of purpose? The Divine? A hallucination? The final creative reflex of a brain deprived of oxygen? I can't answer that for anyone but myself. But I stopped trying to die. And slowly, I came back. The fog lifted. The loud sound returned: the truck's engine, the wind, the soldier beside me shouting, "Pray. Pray!" I couldn't speak, but I nodded, with a faint and tired smile, and began to pray.

We arrived at a nearby town, but the local medics refused to treat us, afraid of retaliation from the guerrilla group in the area. We moved on. Fifteen minutes later, in another town, treatment began. Eventually, a helicopter airlifted three of us to a hospital far away. We were stabilized. I could barely move—tubes in my chest, my body nearly paralyzed. With every attempted movement, I could feel every foreign element inside my body. My mind was quiet, focused only on minimizing pain. A couple of days later, my mother and one of my sisters arrived. Now it was mostly emotion. What I couldn't bear was seeing them walk into the room, place their hands over their mouths, and cry.

It took years before I could fully process what happened that day, not just in memory, but in awareness. I was surviving, reacting; I didn't have the language for it then. But over time, the experience itself revealed its deeper architecture. That moment wasn't only physical, or just emotional, or merely psychological. It wasn't even just spiritual. It was all of them. The body was doing everything it could to survive. The mind was trying to track what had happened, searching for patterns and meaning. I was flooded with a torrent of sensations, thoughts, and emotions that didn't wait for context: anxiety, pain, resolve, acceptance, tenacity, confusion, clarity, trust, and serenity all at once. There was something else—an awareness beyond the story. Not the soldier, not the minister, not the body lying broken; an unconditional presence, untouched by role or belief, simply there. From that observation, a decision arose. Attention turned, intention reoriented.

Sometimes my *Heart* remembers with emotion. Sometimes my *Body* remembers with gratitude. Sometimes my *Mind* remembers with encouragement. Sometimes my *Spirit* remembers to bend, not break. And sometimes, I remember that *I am*. In moments of despair or confusion, when doubt rises or darkness returns, I remember that I didn't go. That moment etched itself into my being, one I no longer need to explain; one I carry still, with gratitude.

The moment was a convergence—felt reality that energy is configured by four *Channels of Experience*. To live with awareness is to recognize how experience is configured, to sense how these channels interact, and to honor the *I Am* that chooses—by directing *attention* and *intention*—how you respond.

The Anatomy of an Experience

To explore *experience*, we begin not with *what* happens, but with *how* it happens through us. I propose *experience* is a dynamic convergence: a moment in which sensation, perception, emotion, and intention co-occur. Something happens around or within you, but it only becomes an *experience* when it is interpreted through your *channels of experience*. It is the internal, moment-to-moment shaping of an event as you live it.

Everything we experience has an energetic character. Consider experience as a living *dance of patterns*; vibration interpreted by awareness, framed by viewpoint and perspective, and directed by attention and intention. From the warmth of the ground beneath your feet to a flicker of thought, life expresses itself through countless rhythms. Experience is the complex interplay of these patterns, tuned and aligned—or at times misaligned—by your Faculties, filters, and intent: adjusting attention as salience (what you amplify), aligning the channels by relative phase (how they stay in sync), and refining the filters through which the moment is perceived.

Experience is not something fixed that arrives fully formed from the outside; it is co-created from within through the four extraordinary channels I've mentioned: *Body*, *Mind*, *Heart*, and *Spirit (attention + intention)*. These aren't anatomical references but symbolic interfaces through which energy is translated into experience. Each channel translates energy in its own way. The *Body* senses. The *Mind* names. The *Heart* amplifies. The *Spirit* guides and multiplies. None operate in isolation; together they form the orchestra of perception.

The channels aren't passive receivers; they are active interpreters, responders, and co-creators.

A Brief Note about Spirit

Before moving on, let me clarify two terms that can sound similar: *spiritual* and *Spirit*. I use *spiritual* to point to a broader sense of connectedness and underlying meaning that some people recognize beneath the surface of life—the quiet context within which our inner life takes shape. For readers who experience this as a pervasive backdrop, that intuition is handled explicitly in this book through the *Nondual Source* (*S*) and the *Outer Field Context*—or, if you prefer a more metaphysical reading, you may think of it as an underlying, field-like backdrop from which the channels seem to take shape. Here, *spiritual* simply names the human recognition of that depth. *Spirit*, by contrast, is the functional principle in this model: the capacity to aim and commit both attention and intention. It is the directional vector of consciousness, the inner compass that decides *where* and *why* you focus. Like "the spirit of ingenuity" or "the spirit of inquiry," it is the guiding presence behind action, bringing your inner system into coherence through focus rather than force.

The *Four Channels of Experience* weave together often faster than thought. Recall receiving a message that surprises you: your *Body* feels a jolt of adrenaline, your *Mind* races to interpret, your *Heart* swells with excitement or anxiety, and your *Spirit* either scatters focus or gathers presence. Experience is this symphony in motion—*sensation, cognition, emotion,* and *will* playing as one field.

To make sense of this orchestration, we can observe its inner architecture. What follows is not a scientific equation, but a reflective tool. One way to express it is:

$$\mathbf{E = (\mathit{B} + \mathit{M} + \mathit{H}) \times \mathit{S}}$$

- ***B* = Body — The Physical Tuning Fork**: Registers raw sensory data—temperature, texture, tension, motion. Sensations (sight, hearing, smell, taste, and touch) aren't mere reflexes; they're information that gains meaning once the *Mind* interprets them.
- ***M* = Mind — The Narrative Architect**: Organizes sensation into concepts, creating frames, names, interpretations, and stories. Neutral input becomes charged only when the *Mind* frames it.

- *H* = **Heart — The Emotional Resonator**: The resonant amplifier of tone and depth. While *Body* and *Mind* provide data and narrative, the *Heart* colors experience as emotion (which the *Mind* labels as happiness, fear, anger, etc.), so the same situation can move one person to tears and another to numbness.
- *S* = **Spirit (attention + intention) — The Guiding Compass, multiplier, and integrator**: Your *attention* decides which moments you amplify or overlook; your *intention* shapes how you engage what you notice. *Spirit* aligns attention and intention, amplifying what matters and integrating the channels so chosen possibilities crystallize.

The expression $(B + M + H) \times S$ describes the full inner-shaping of experience—each indispensable, each interacting to shape how life is experienced in any given moment. Too much *M* with little *S* leads to over-analysis, or strong *H* with weak *S* may result in being lost in emotion. When the *Mind* rushes to label, it can mask the *Heart's* raw resonance. That mislabeling then spills into the *Body* as tension and scatters *Spirit's* attention away from its intended aim. Two people may feel the same bodily pain (*B*) and assign the same story to it (*M*), but if one meets it with focused presence and the other with resistance, their lived experiences will diverge entirely.

Experience is inseparable from time and space. The *Mind* measures time in sequence (though that sequence is an interpreted chain of *now*-moments), the *Heart* anchors significance, the *Body* responds to motion, and *Spirit (attention + intention)* stretches a single breath into timelessness or compresses a year into a blur.

Outer context supplies the canvas; inner configuration paints the picture. This reveals two complementary dynamics shaping every moment. First is the **Inner Shaping Dynamic**, where your Body's sensations (*B*), your Mind's meaning-making (*M*), and your heart's emotional resonance (*H*) are sculpted by your attention and intention (*S*). This is how you shape experience from within. Second is the **Outer Field Context** (this sits outside the inner expression; it simply provides the external inputs you then interpret). It encompasses the surrounding context—your physical environment and social dynamics. It is not a variable in the formula; it influences inputs, but never determines outcomes, since outcomes depend on the *Inner Shaping Dynamic.* While $(B + M + H) \times S$ captures your *Inner Shaping Dynamic,* the *Outer Field Context* supplies the changing conditions your inner system tunes to. Your experience is always a dynamic blend of both.

Every experience you've ever had wasn't simply about what occurred. It is the interplay of the Four Channels. Most importantly, what you live through may become entangled with who you believe yourself to be, but the one who sees it all unconditionally and impartially—your *I Am*—remains untethered.

Once an experience is formed, how do you interpret it? The words we use—especially the six Wh-Words—act as coordinates that position our awareness. They interpret what manifests. Let's explore them in their lived form.

You and the 6 Wh-Words

Experience Shaped by Language

The six Wh-Words—*What, Why, Where, When, How,* and *Who*—actively organize your lived reality. They are more than questions; they are frameworks of perception. In this context, when we use the word *live,* we are speaking about the *living* of experience, not the question of existence itself. The focus is on how you move through your experiences and how language reveals or distorts what you perceive. The way you engage each of these words often springs from a deeper blueprint—your core patterns of moving between trust and control, or courage and fear.

The precision of the questions we ask often matters more than the answers themselves. Clarity often begins by asking: *What am I doing to myself, to others, or what is being done to me? What am I doing with this?* Each Wh-Word offers a distinct entry point into awareness. *Why* touches the currents of meaning. *Where* locates the context of your experience. *How* reveals your method of engagement. *When* situates your presence in time. *What* sharpens your focus on the moment's form. And *Who* invites you to recognize the presence you are embodying.

Experience is lived, but it is also built. Language is the blueprint. In Chapter 3 we named the Wh-Words; here we *live* them. In the sections that follow, we will explore how *living* each of these words can bring greater coherence to the architecture of your experience.

Living Your Why

The Current of Meaning and Motivation Behind Experience
Experiences rarely emerge at random; they're shaped by visible and hidden intents. Your *Why* is the chosen *reason* you move—what you are aiming to serve or reveal in a given moment. To live your *Why* is to recognize the currents already moving within you: the meanings you assign, the reason for the directions you choose, and the identities you reinforce. When awareness meets intention, experience becomes an opportunity for refinement and design.

> Living Your Why *is compassionately recognizing the intent that animates every action.*

Quick Reminder: *Living Your Why*—as with your *When*, *How*, and *Where*—is all about your intrinsic capacity to create and manifest experience. For example, an isolated *why* can evoke causation outside of your control. Someone else's decision can expose you to an unintended event. Although you may still shape your reaction, these sections focus on your inner, configurable experience. Naming a *Why* clarifies your *intentionality*; it doesn't claim you caused the entire event.

Throughout depression, I lived a *why* strictly from judgment—trying to reconcile every situation through *frames* outside my control. Narratives evoking natural laws of a misrepresented "karma-like" perspective: blaming myself or others. In Chapter 3, I wrote: "When answering 'Why Are you?', the answer may be as simple as 'Because I can,' then deciding what is appropriate and conducive to your conscious aspiration."

Living Your Why reclaims authorship to write the next chapters of your life. It often begins with noticing how easily questions misalign with a true need for clarity. By realigning the question, you can unlock a deeper layer of understanding.

Situation	Default Pattern	Awareness-Infused "Why"
A plan is delayed.	"When will this finally be over?"	"Why is completing this important to me?"
Doubting a relationship.	"Where did things go wrong?"	"Why do I feel disconnected right now?"
Feeling stuck in a decision.	"How can I fix this immediately?"	"Why am I hesitating to choose?"
Experiencing rejection.	"Who is to blame for this?"	"Why does this outcome matter so much to me?"
Maintaining motivation.	"What could I be doing differently?"	"Why did I begin this journey in the first place?"

Checking your Why isn't self-blame; it's self-location.
The shift is subtle but powerful. By asking *Why* with *honesty*, you re-center your experience on meaning and motivation. When the motive shifts, the same action expresses a different *Why*. *Why* is the silent force behind choice and endurance. The clearer the meaning and motivation, the clearer you direct your experience.

As you uncover your *Why*, you may notice some are tied to the persona—the roles you've learned to perform—with hidden layers of unconscious identity, conditioning, or even fear. Returning to your *I Am* restores the axis of true choice. To *live your Why* is to remember *who* is moving within the experience, not just what the experience demands.

Reflection

- When something stirs strong emotion, pause and ask: "What *Why* is being activated in me?"
- When you find yourself frustrated or exhausted, ask: "Is the *Why* I am living truly mine, or is it inherited?"
- When clarity or peace arises, notice: "What hidden alignment of intention is now revealed?"
- When you hear yourself ask, "Why do I keep doing this?", pause. Ask instead: "What am I actually doing right now?"

Living Your Why is not about solving or taming experience. It is about recognizing meaning and motivation as a living current—one you can meet with awareness, refine with honesty, and align with authenticity. The more you live your *Why* from conscious awareness, the more each experience, even in uncertainty, becomes a doorway back to yourself. But meaning and motivation don't exist in a vacuum. Now let's move to *Living Your Where*—within you, in relation to others, or in the field around you.

Living Your Where

The Positioning of Experience
Experiences carry a felt position. To live your *Where* is to recognize where your awareness situates within an experience; the stance you hold and the direction of your focus. Your *Where* is not a place outside you; it is the *inner position* from which you perceive and participate.

While often thought of as a place outside you—a city, a room, a situation—in lived experience, *Where* is much closer. It is your position within the flow of the moment. The key question is: "Where am I standing internally as this emerges?" Each experience places you somewhere on a spectrum between trust and fear, expansion and contraction, or connection and isolation. The experience itself has not defined you, but *where* you hold it defines how you live it.

This positioning also applies to our relationships. Experiences do not occur in isolation; they're configured in relation to others, to events, and to versions of yourself. *Living Your Where* means noticing this relational stance: "Where am I standing in relation to this person?" "Where am I between judgment and understanding?" This is a subtle yet powerful awareness that can reinforce separation or open pathways for authentic connection.

Your perceived *Where* directly shapes your Viewpoint (what enters the frame) and your Perspective (how you interpret it). *Where* (inner stance) biases Viewpoint (Stage 5 selection), which Perspective then narrates; Attention collapses the choice into action (Stage 5→6).

A narrow internal placement narrows the field of vision, while an expansive one widens it. *Living Your Where* invites a conscious shift, allowing you to ask, "Am I looking at this from a place of confinement or from a place of possibility?" Remember: *Where* names an inner stance, not a value judgment.

Channel	Primary Function in "Where"
Body	*Registers placement somatically*
Mind	*Frames and labels* placement
Heart	*Resonates with placement and modulates openness/closure*
Spirit (attention + intention)	*Orients placement* (aim & direction)

Living Your Where asks for a fuller listening—to sense this entire architecture of experience. It dissolves the rigidity of dualistic thinking and repositions you within the flowing polarities of awareness. This awareness allows for practical shifts in how we frame our position:

Default Pattern	Awareness-Infused "Where"
"Where did everything fall apart?" (fixed loss)	"Where am I now between the disintegration of the old and the emergence of the new?"
"Where is the perfect outcome I needed?" (idealism trap)	"Where am I in this moment, even if it is incomplete?"

Reflection

Living Your Where begins within—but it does not end there. Experience unfolds not only in your inner landscape but also in *relation* to the Outer Field Context. Bringing awareness to the external *Where* helps you notice how the environment influences what is registered and how it is lived.

Consider asking yourself:

- **Plane:** Which plane is primary here—Physical, Astral (emotional/imaginal), Mental, or Causal?
- **Density:** What density is salient—denser/contracted to subtler/expansive?

- **Realm:** Which expression domain is most active—Material (behavior/embodiment), Emotional/Imaginal (affect & imagery), Intellectual (concepts/meaning-making), or Noetic/Transpersonal?
- **Dimension:** What dimensional framing am I in—3D + time sequence or a non-linear/atemporal awareness?

Quick check: Where am I (stance), what am I seeing (viewpoint), and what story am I making (perspective)?

Consider these as practical lenses that help you notice the different layers shaping your experience. Noticing these external qualifiers of *Where* can reveal why an experience might feel heavy in one setting and fluid in another, sharp in one moment and soft in another. Environment amplifies or attenuates experience—but it does not dictate your awareness. By living both your inner and outer *Where*, you navigate experience with greater clarity, coherence, and conscious participation. Hermann Hesse writes in *Siddhartha*:

> *"...the river is everywhere at once, at the source and at the mouth, at the waterfall, at the ferry, at the rapids, in the sea, in the mountains, everywhere at once, and that there is only the present time for it, not the shadow of the past, not the shadow of the future."*[4]

Like *Siddhartha* listening to the river, wisdom lies not only in noticing where we stand within the flow, but in realizing the river is its entirety—source and mouth, calm and turbulence, all at once. The river reminds us that *Living Your Where* is about conscious engagement. To know your *Where* is to locate a point on your inner map of experience, navigate in real time, and recognize your freedom in how experience is lived. It offers orientation, and while it may suggest a direction, you still choose *how* to move. We now turn to the quality of the journey itself: the method, rhythm, and unique signature of your engagement—*Living Your How*.

---

4 Hermann Hesse, *Siddhartha: A New Translation*, trans. Joachim Neugroschel (New York: Penguin Books, 1999), 166

Living Your How

The Method of Engagement

Experiences are shaped not only by what happens, but by *how* you move through them. The difference isn't *what* is done—it's *how*. *How* is the *living impression on each moment*. While the experience may be shared, the *How* you bring to it is uniquely yours.

> Living Your How *is the living imprint of presence —the signature by which you meet experience.*

A child tried to gain his mother's attention to share an exciting story. His mother was busy, and the child was frustrated because he felt his mom wasn't listening. Mom said: "I'm listening." The child responded, "Listen to me with your eyes."[5] *How* exposes your method of engagement. Do you operate on autopilot, or do you participate in every moment? Do you move with creative openness, or grip with defensive control? *Living Your How* means noticing these internal architectures before they build entire realities from unseen foundations.

Many of the difficulties we encounter stem less from *why* or *what* happened and more from *how* we lived the experience. It is not only the decision you made or what you did, but the *way* you do it; not only the words you spoke, but the manner you infused into them. *Living Your How* invites a deeper reflection: *Am I participating with full presence?*

Channel	"How" Is Expressed Through
Body	Posture, movement, and pace
Mind	Narrative, strategy, process, and mental framing
Heart	Emotional openness, resonance, or contraction
Spirit (attention + intention)	Clarity of focus or diffusion/scatter of aim

5 Ana Veciana-Suarez, "Listen to me with your eyes!" *The Miami Herald*, May 21, 1989, 1G.

Sometimes the *Body* moves with grace, but the *Mind* spins with doubt. Sometimes your *Heart* calls to resonate with happiness, but your attention drifts. Recognizing this full choreography reveals how experience *is engagement* at every level of your being, but it may not always align with clear attention or coherent intention. The quality of this engagement is mostly energized by attention and oriented by intention. When attention to the process is sharp, the signature of every engagement is no longer a scribble, but an intentional trace of your actions. This awareness allows you to shift your engagement consciously:

Default Pattern	Awareness-Infused "How"
Performing in autopilot	Flowing with intentional presence
Reacting automatically	Choosing deliberate engagement
Rushing to outcomes	Living the process as it occurs

Each subtle shift in *how* alters the experience you live. The thread of *How* runs through every model of experience we explore. For instance, a *how* lived from your core *I Am* presence brings effortless alignment, while a *how* lived from habit or persona often feels fragmented.

Reflection

Begin with this question: *How am I shaping or framing this experience?* Then, consider these examples:

Initial Intent (Why/What)	Question (how)	Statement of Process (How)
"I care about others' opinions."	"How am I listening to others?"	"I pause before reacting and listen without interruption."
"I don't want to be hurt."	"How am I protecting while staying open?"	"I allow space for dialogue but set boundaries."
"I want to live a healthy life."	"How am I improving my health?"	"I walk every morning and follow a tailored nutrition plan."
"I am driven."	"How am I actualizing motivation?"	"I actively focus and act."

Each *How* is an expression of your *Faculties* and *Channels of Experience* at work—*Body* embodying, *Mind* framing, *Heart* resonating, *Spirit* orienting. By illuminating your *How*, you consciously configure experience and prepare the next stages of the *Flow of Existence* by effectively tracing the imprints of your *How*.

Living Your How transforms experience, from mere intent or hope for an outcome, into conscious participation. It is not only *what* you experience in life; it is *how* you engage in life's experiences. From the method you bring, we turn to its timing: *Living Your When*.

Living Your When

The Dimension of Timing

We learn to dance with the perception of time rather than trying to control it. *Living Your When* is more than a timestamp; it is the living tempo of experience, with a pulse that emerges, expands, and recedes according to its own inner timing.

> Living Your When *is not just referencing a clock—it is the rhythm of awareness shaping how you perceive time.*

You feel it when a conversation deepens naturally instead of being rushed, when grief needs more time to soften than you expected, or when inspiration arrives not by force, but because the moment is ready. *Living Your When* means attuning to this pulse—not racing ahead of it or dragging behind it, but moving with it.

Your relationship with *When* is also influenced by core patterns that live between *courage* and *fear*, *trust* and *control*, *patience* and *urgency*. Each moment reveals whether you are in step with the experience or trying to pull it into your preferred tempo. Courage evokes trust; trust allows for emergence. Fear rushes or freezes; control demands immediacy. When you meet life through these dualities, you realize it is not time you need to flex, but your own capacity to be present within it. A clear example is feeling the urgency to move into a romantic relationship immediately, even when an inner knowing whispers that something is incomplete.

Living Your When means honoring the wisdom of ripening instead of bowing to the pressure of haste.

Sometimes we encounter moments contextualized and amplified by a remembered story or a future, *fabulous* one. Both pull you out of the living pulse of the actual moment. Clinging to a memory as if it is happening again (or will), not only blinds you to what is happening now, but it is illusory because no moment repeats itself, and every conscious experience is always new. It is fascinating to realize that what we experience is always *now.*

We are masterful storytellers, constructing entire emotional worlds around memories or imagined futures. Sometimes the strongest feeling in a moment is not what is happening, but the story we have written about it. For example, we might feel betrayed by someone based not on their actual actions, but on a narrative we've spun about their unseen motives. *Living Your When* invites you to notice: *Am I living this moment, or inhabiting a script I wrote without re-reading?*

Channel	"When" Is Expressed Through
Body	Sensations of pace, fatigue, and readiness
Mind	Narratives of urgency, timing, and regret
Heart	Emotional currents of anticipation, longing, and hesitation
Spirit (attention + intention)	Synchronization (or mismatch) of aim with the moment's tempo.

Your lived relationship to any moment is shaped by choice, focus, and intention in the *now*. You cannot change past events, but you can change how you experience the past now. You cannot guarantee the future, but you can shape how you prepare for the future now. *Living Your When* means reclaiming today as the gateway where all experience exists. It restores coherence to the way past and future influence the present.

Default Pattern	Awareness-Infused "When"
Rushing outcomes	Configuring in real-time
Clinging to past moments	Meeting the living present
Forcing future projections	Cultivating present intentionality

Each choice transports you back either into or out of step with every experience. Your awareness of *When*—whether you feel too early, too late, or perfectly timed—directly positions your Viewpoint. With urgency, you see life as scarce and pressured. With regret, you see a life filled with missed chances. With presence, you see life as living potential. This awareness allows you to shift your relationship with time. Possibilities you thought didn't exist appear like rays of sunlight as the clouds disappear.

Reflection

Use these questions to attune to the living rhythm of your experience:

- When you feel a strong impulse to rush a decision or force an outcome, pause and ask: "What natural tempo am I resisting right now?"
- You've probably said it before: "I'll be happy when..." But *When* isn't later. It's the rhythm with a melody and lyrics you're living *now*.
- When a memory of regret or a past success surfaces strongly, ask: "Am I using this memory as a tool for insight, or as a memory to re-live?"
- Where in your body do you feel the pressure of urgency or the weight of the past? Can you breathe into that sensation without needing it to change?
- What is one small choice you can make today to align yourself with the timing of what is, rather than the timing you believe it should be?

Recognizing *when* your awareness dwells—in the past, future, or the vibrant now—gives you power over the rhythm of your life. We have explored the *why* of your intent, the *where* of your position, the *how* of your engagement, and the *when* as your relationship with time. Now, we turn our focus to the substance of the moment itself: what is being lived in that moment—*Living Your What*.

Living Your What

The Substance of Experience

Every moment you live carries a *What—the living substance* of what you are feeling, choosing, and embodying through attention and intention. *What* is more than something that happens to you; it is *what* you bring alive—what you focus on, what you energize through thought and emotion, and what you shape through intention or default.

> *Your* What *is the raw substance of life you energize—whether by choice or by default.*

The substance you embody reflects the core patterns of your being and the polarities you navigate between, such as Authentic Self and persona, or consonance and dissonance. Misalignment often shows itself when the *What* you live contradicts your deeper knowing. You may achieve outward success, yet feel inner hollowness because what you embodied was fueled by fear of inadequacy rather than joy or purpose. *Living Your What* asks for honesty: *Is what I am living aligned with my I Am, or am I chasing a projection?*

Channel	"What" Is Expressed Through
Body	Sensation, movement, gestures, action
Mind	Meaning, interpretation, attribution, imagination
Heart	Consonance or dissonance
Spirit (attention + intention)	Clarity of a formed and intended outcome

Living Your What is also deeply influenced by Perception, Viewpoint, and Perspective. Like the examples of stepping on an ant in *Chapter 4: What Are You?* or the cylinder in *Chapter 6: True vs Truth*, *What* you experience is very often labeled and boxed as a single formed outcome, a single manifestation. But an outcome isn't boxed with a shipping label, even if we try to frame it as such, ignoring the formulation of an experience.

I was once in an online meeting, and my laptop suddenly froze. I could only hear the audio of the meeting conductor, but not her video. Fortunately, one of my sisters was holding the meeting and kindly waited for me. Frustration grew, and I began complaining *to the computer* as if it had chosen to reincarnate from its nightmarish counterparts of the late 90's. As I pounded on the keyboard, remembering bygone years when old operating systems would just stop working, name-calling the new laptop seemed my only way out. A few minutes after the meeting had to end, I realized the Bluetooth signal was still on and the connection with the mouse in my backpack was still in effect after a long flight. The way the backpack was set on the floor was compressing the mouse and sending a signal back, like a permanent click. The mouse and the laptop worked exactly as designed. But what I remembered—*Living a When*—and a hidden *Why* became the focus of the problem. It was almost like an unsolved mystery of a supposed plot between the ghosts of the old laptops and the new one to disrupt my very important meeting. All my energy went into frustration. Silly! I embodied frustration, grievance, and drama—an unnecessary creative act. I energized frustration (H), told a blame story (M), tightened posture/breath (B), and scattered attention (S).

Just as the past and future are only experienced today as memory or imagination, so too is your *What*. The *When* marks tempo, but the *What* is the substance you energize in that tempo. You live *what* you focus on *now*. Observe. Assign meaning. Recognize structure. You cannot live a different yesterday, but you can live a different *What* today by shifting or reinforcing the statement of meaning in the present moment. This is not to suggest drawing up illusions or lying, but to seek clarity and expand knowledge. It allows you to shift from a default pattern to an awareness-infused state:

Default Pattern	Awareness-Infused "What"
Living assumptions	Living from present conscious choice
Enacting old wounds	Embodying present possibilities
Reacting from haste	Acting from coherence and clarity

With each choice of *What*, you weave your lived experience into the tapestry of reality. You are not merely a witness—you are its active shaper. Awareness is the loom; choice is the thread. *Living Your What* is living consciously. It is remembering that every breath, every focus, every feeling is part of the reality you are shaping—now, and always.

Reflection

The *What* of your experience is the substance you are living. When you catch yourself using identity-based or purely emotional labels, pause and ask: "What is the actual *what* of this moment—what is being done, felt, or shaped right now?" Here is how to translate into a simple, literal, observable *What*:

- "I'm productive." may just be "I'm typing on my laptop."
- "I'm good." may just be "I'm holding the door for someone."
- "I'm ruined." may just be "I'm facing difficulty and can't find an alternate route."
- "I'm stressed." may just be "I'm drinking alcohol excessively."
- "I'm a connected being." may just be "I'm walking barefoot on grass."

Recognizing what you focus on, ask: "What substance—what quality of being—am I energizing right now?" Then ask: "Do I color it with gratitude, curiosity, openness?" Before entering a challenging situation, ask yourself: "What do I intend to bring into this space—what quality, what expression, what energetic tone?"

We have now explored the full architecture of our lived moments: the *why* of our intent, the *where* of our position, the *how* of our engagement, the *when* of our timing, and the *what* of our embodied substance. We now turn our focus from the experience itself to the one who experiences—*Living Your Who*.

Living Your Who

The Experiencing Presence

Experiences are defined by the awareness that lives through them—the *Who* behind every moment. This *I Am* is the unwavering experiencer, the still presence behind every action, emotion, and perception. Personas, roles, and identities are merely filters as this awareness engages with the world. For example, a critical comment at work may feel crushing or neutral, depending on which internal filter—"the one who must be perfect" versus "the one learning and evolving"—is active. To live your *Who* is to recognize: *I am not the filter; I am the living awareness engaging through it.*

> Living Your Who *is not about a role to perform; it is about the authentic presence only you can embody.*

Your emotional reality is determined by this same dynamic. No external event can inject anger, peace, or happiness into you. External events may catalyze emotional states, but they do not install them. Your system configures what becomes your lived emotion. A friend's silence could spark anxiety in one moment and a sense of grateful peace in another, depending on the *who you assign* within you.

While stimuli may spark responses, the collapse of that potential into a lived experience often remains your sovereign choice; when capacity is overwhelmed, rebuilding choice begins with restoring safety and presence. This reveals your authority and autonomy. A lack of clarity about your inner state may cloud your perception, but the authority to choose your response always remains. *Living Your Who* means reclaiming leadership over the vibrational field you embody, like choosing patience over defensiveness, not because the situation dictates it, but because you exercised your choice consciously.

Channel	"Who" Is Expressed Through
Body	Felt presence, movement, and action rhythms
Mind	Identity narratives, assumptions, and inner dialogues
Heart	Emotional coloring and resonance with experience
Spirit (attention + intention)	Aim, focus, and engagement of will

Your viewpoint acts as the tuning lens for *Who*. From a constricted viewpoint, you identify with roles like *the one who is wronged* or *the one who must be right*. From an expanded viewpoint, you sense yourself as fluid awareness. Polarity reminds you that you are not fixed between extremes like *victim* and *victimizer* or *reactive* and *responsive*. You are not locked in a single self-definition; these are states, not identities; you move across them by choice and awareness. Awareness allows you to live as a fluid, *authentic self* rather than a rigid persona or a wounded role.

Who you are is not lived in the past or constructed in the future; it is experienced *now*. Recognizing that in this moment, you can live as *the one who adapts* is how you rewrite your vibrational experience by choice. You shift from absorbing emotional contagion to choosing your internal response.

You are not passively assigned an identity. You are the living architect of how awareness vibrates through the field of experience. Your *Faculties* (Stage 4) allow your *Who* to evolve after every *Feedback Loop* (Stage 7), with *Spirit (attention+intention)* re-aiming the vector each loop, tuning your *Authority* to lead your vibrational expression, and your *Autonomy* as the freedom to choose from where you live your *Who*, moment by moment.

Living Your Who is living awake. It is remembering that identity is an imagined character, a vibrational canvas. Every breath, every choice is another brushstroke of the *Who* you live into reality. You are not the story. *You are the living author*.

But every author works with a structure, a blueprint from which creation takes form. Having met the author—the *Who* at the center—we now turn to the very blueprint they use. Let us explore the *Architecture of Your Experience*.

Living the Architecture of Your Experience

Experience is a living architecture, shaped moment by moment through how we question, frame, and meet it. Every lived moment carries dimensions that can be illuminated by the six Wh-Words. Let's recap:

- **Why** brings meaning and motive into view.
- **Where** reveals positioning and context.
- **How** shapes the manner of engagement.
- **When** attunes to timing and readiness.
- **What** names the substance of your focus.
- **Who** centers the awareness that lives through it all.

Experience becomes clearer when awareness navigates these dimensions skillfully. Often, clarity feels elusive because our attention anchors in a dimension that cannot resolve the tension. We might seek *Why* too early when *What* or *How* needs attention first, or focus on *Where* when the real tension is *When*. The art of awareness is sensing where to inquire, not just asking out of habit. Choosing a formulation with care invites a distinct reality.

Habitual vs. Awareness-Expanding Formulations:

Habitual Question	Awareness-Expanding Formulation
Why can't I get this right?	What am I practicing through this challenge?
Where did I go wrong?	How am I meeting what is arising now?
How could they treat me that way?	Who within me is responding to this experience?
When will I finally arrive?	What is available to live here and now?

Experiences often evolve through a natural sequence of Wh-Word shifts. Consider an opportunity arising. The sequence might transpire like this: you first connect with **Meaning** (*Why does this resonate with me?*), then with **Positioning** (*Where do I feel called to move?*). From there, you explore the **Manner** of engagement (*How am I approaching this?*), the **Timing** (*When feels aligned for action?*), the **Substance** (*What am I living through this decision?*), and finally, the **Presence** leading the movement (*Who within me is leading?*).

Formulating a living question is more than choosing a word; it is the art of arranging your attention and clarifying your intention to open space for new configurations. When you formulate a question, you are making dynamic moves across several layers: where you place your **attention** (mental and emotional focus) and **intention** (Why you are engaging with the experience), how you

frame the inquiry, the emotional **tone** you bring, and the **identity position** you are asking from. When unconscious, these dynamics create habitual patterns. When conscious, they become tools for liberation.

Consider the shift from a habitual to a conscious formulation in a few scenarios:

Scenario: A Career Transition
Habitual Unconscious Formulation: "Why can't I figure out what I want?"

- Attention: on failure and lack
- Intention: to fix a perceived problem
- Framing: limiting, narrow
- Tone: frustration
- Identity: disempowered self-image

Living Conscious Formulation: "What am I ready to explore with curiosity?"

- Attention: on emerging possibilities
- Intention: to open discovery
- Framing: expansive
- Tone: compassion and courage
- Identity: resilient creator

Scenario: Emotional Overwhelm
Habitual Unconscious Formulation: "Why do people always treat me this way?"

- Attention: external blame
- Intention: justify suffering
- Framing: fixed victimhood
- Tone: resentment
- Identity: wounded role

Living Conscious Formulation: "Where am I anchoring my sense of worth?"

- Attention: inward responsibility
- Intention: empowerment
- Framing: self-inquiry and possibility

- Tone: gentleness
- Identity: autonomous self-expression

Scenario: A Creative Block
Habitual Unconscious Formulation: "How come nothing ever flows for me?"

- Attention: scarcity and frustration
- Intention: evidence-seeking for limitation
- Framing: helplessness
- Tone: despair
- Identity: self-limiting persona

Living Conscious Formulation: "How can I create a space for inspiration to arise naturally?"

- Attention: present possibility
- Intention: collaboration with emergence
- Framing: empowerment and flow
- Tone: openness
- Identity: creator rather than controller

When a question arises automatically, it is often shaped by your emotional state (Am I framing from fear, hope, anger, gratitude?), your hidden beliefs (What assumptions am I carrying about myself, others, or life?), your viewpoint constraints (Is my lens constricted, or am I seeing from expanded awareness?), or the voices you've inherited from your past (Am I formulating through voices inherited from parents, teachers, culture—or from my *Authentic Self*?).

There is no shame in noticing an old pattern. Identifying a formulation shaped by anger is an act of expansion, not a sign of failure. Recognizing an inherited story is a moment of reclaimed Mastery. Offer yourself compassion when you catch an old form surfacing. Every conscious shift is already a movement into greater awareness and free and unconditioned expression.

Your experience is a living structure. No moment is random. Each question you live feeds the experience you shape, and each experience reshapes the questions you are ready to ask. This is a living *Feedback Loop*—a dance of questioning, experiencing, and evolving. There is no last question, only deeper ways to meet being's architecture. You may inherit architectures built by others, but you are the living architect and builder of *your own field*, breath by breath, choice by choice. Living the architecture of your experience means skillfully using the language of awareness to navigate your inner world.

We have now mapped the blueprint. Now, let's turn our attention to the very materials from which this architecture is built and the process of tuning and attuning the four fundamental channels that interpret and co-create the raw data of experience.

Tuning and Attuning Your Four Channels of Experience

Your *Four Channels of Experience* are already on and active. You do not have to turn them on or off. The invitation is to participate with growing clarity. With careful attention to your channels, you can transition from disassociation to devoted attention, with the goal of appreciating the beauty of the Body's signals, the Mind's patterns, the Heart's resonances, and the Spirit's focused intent, treating them as a living garden. Sometimes the Body tenses because it longs for stillness; sometimes it expands because it recognizes safety. As if asking to be heard, each channel carries its own energetic, tonal signature.

To bring practical clarity to this process, I refer to your real-time capacity to notice and refine your Channels of Experience as the *Channel-Quotients*. *Tuning* is sensing and refining each channel individually. *Attuning* is bringing them into resonance with each other and with your present context. I will refer to each Channel-Quotient as: Channel Physical Quotient (CPQ), Channel Inquiry Quotient (CIQ), Channel Empathy Quotient (CEQ), and Channel Alignment Quotient (CAQ). Borrowing the "-Q" shorthand from education, psychology, and wellness, each Channel-Quotient is less a score and more a literacy: your living capacity to notice, tune, and refine the signals each channel contributes to experience.

Body | Physical Tuning Fork

Last 100 Meters: Step by Step

I had been selected alongside two highly trained squads to reach a communications post positioned atop one of the tallest peaks in the region. A large repeater antenna stationed there was critical for relaying signals to troops below. My role in the mission was technical: to draw up defensive perimeter plans. I was new, with barely a month of field service. This was my first long expedition.

We began our ascent from the lowlands, marching for hours. The initial stretch was manageable, but as the slope increased, so did the weight of my gear, or at least, how it felt. My body strained with every step. Stopping wasn't an option; we were too exposed and had to reach our destination before nightfall. By the tenth hour, the summit felt unreachable. The others moved with practiced ease. I had dropped to the back of the group, and they could see I was struggling.

One of the experienced soldiers dropped back and walked beside me. He didn't rush or reprimand. He just coached me on how to regulate my breathing and sync my steps with it. He spoke of pace and rhythm, and how to stop racing against a mountain that wasn't going anywhere. Of everything he said, one piece stayed with me: "The closer we get, the harder it feels. That's normal. Don't look up. Think of a song. Keep your rhythm. Focus on each step. Maintain your pace. Don't think about when we'll arrive. Just breathe and step."

I followed his voice. I let go of the peak and kept moving. The slope grew steeper, like climbing a staircase carved into the mountain itself. Then word came: just a hundred meters to go. I looked up and saw the base, but those last hundred meters felt like a hundred kilometers. The closer I got, the more distant it appeared. He stepped back down a few paces and calmly reminded me, "Don't look up. Just hear my voice. Focus on each step. Then the next. Steady."

So I did. Step by step. Until I arrived. I didn't reach the top with a burst of strength. I arrived because I stopped resisting the climb. I listened, regulated, and aligned. The body tires, the mind resists, and emotions stir. Possibility shifts only when Body, Mind, Heart, and Spirit begin to align. Sometimes, we don't overcome the mountain. We just stop fighting it, and that's what lets us arrive.

In those final hundred meters, something essential became clear. Each step carried more than weight; it carried attention. As rhythm returned, so did a relationship with my body. It wasn't just moving through terrain; it was translating the moment into breath, pressure, and balance. That shift marked the beginning of awareness lived through form.

Experience emerges simultaneously with all four channels, but the body gives it physical shape, pace, and pulse. It's tempting to treat the body as something we *have* or *are*, rather than as a channel that actively shapes physical experience. "Feeling good" lives in the curve of your smile. Calm slows your breathing and eases muscle tension. The body doesn't merely reflect what is happening; it participates in shaping it with immediacy and honesty. You don't need a diagnosis to know your shoulders are carrying too much. The body is already speaking. The question is, are you listening?

Your body is the living antenna that picks up vibrations as raw sensory data. Your mind, by contrast, is the storyteller and interpreter; co-arises with and organizes signals—from the body, memory, symbol, and imagination—into meaning. While the brain (and arguably other physical organs) stores memories and processes neural impulses, the mind is the dance of ideas, concepts, and narratives that arise as you make sense of those impulses. Think of it like this: *Body* is the resonant soundboard that turns vibration into audible tone; *Mind* is the arranger that scores those tones into a coherent piece. Keeping them distinct helps you notice when you're simply reacting to a sensation and when you're interpreting it.

Your **Channel Physical Quotient (CPQ)**—your ability to listen to and work with your body in real time—reflects the clarity of your Body's participation in every lived experience with its own *feedback loops*: breath, posture, physical feeling, balance, and rhythm. A muted or misread body signal affects everything that follows. The *Heart* may feel overwhelmed, the *Mind* fills in the blanks with interpretation, and the *Spirit*'s focus becomes harder to steady. But when physical awareness sharpens, the entire system coheres.

The *Body* is the primary channel in continuous contact with the physical world; a natural synchronizer for the other channels' timing and load. When CPQ is clear, the rest of your system can resonate, interpret, and align more freely.

Practices for Refining CPQ (Physical Tuning)
To deepen your CPQ, treat your body as a collaborative instrument rather than a machine to be fixed.

- **Move intentionally.** Engage in playful movement like morning stretches or dancing. This awakens the physical interface and primes your mind for creativity and presence.
- **Strengthen foundations.** Short, focused bouts of resistance or cardio send corrective feedback to your nervous system, rebuilding trust in your body's capacity to respond and adapt.
- **Listen through breath.** A single conscious, slightly longer exhale can activate a parasympathetic response and open a channel to inner awareness, grounding you in the present.
- **Nourish and rest well.** Rhythm, nourishment, and recovery regulate your physical systems, preserving a stable baseline so the other channels don't have to compensate for physical dysregulation.

You don't need a full ritual to "reconnect." A few seconds of attention can restore clarity in real time:

- **Ground through the five senses.** Actively notice what you are hearing, feeling, smelling, tasting, and seeing. This instantly reduces mental chatter and focuses awareness into your body.
- **Perform a somatic sweep.** A quick head-to-toe scan cultivates awareness. Where is tension gathering? Where can you soften by even 10%? This sends feedback that you can influence your own physiological state.
- **Use a breath cue.** Inhale for four counts; exhale for six (longer exhale increases vagal tone). Offer your body—and the rest of you—a reminder with kindness,

love, and compassion: "We're here now." This reinforces the mind-body Feedback Loop.

Together, these techniques build somatic literacy—the skill of reading and responding to your *Body's* signals so you can course-correct before stress patterns crystallize. Tuning into your CPQ doesn't require you to master every sensation. It invites you to stay in relationship with what your form is already translating. In honoring your *Body*, you return to the living architecture of awareness.

But this physical interface is in constant dialogue with the other channels. We now turn our attention from the physical to the cognitive, to explore the second channel: *Mind.*

Mind | Narrative Architect

The Internal Premiere

It starts with a look—barely a glance, really. You're mid-conversation, or passing someone familiar. There's a pause in their tone, a flicker in their expression you didn't expect. And suddenly, the mind steps in. A whole internal feature film begins production:

- *Scene One:* They're upset.
- *Scene Two:* You've (or they have) must have done something wrong.
- *Scene Three:* A full cast of imagined reactions fills the stage.

You haven't moved, but inside, the narrative unfolds as the *Mind* goes into motion, writing scripts, directing emotions, and casting you in multiple roles, all from a single perceived cue. Later, you learn they were just preoccupied or tired. The story loosens its grip. And in the stillness that follows, something becomes clear: the *Mind* is a meaning-maker. Your ability to notice this process in motion—how quickly stories are drafted—is the essence of your **Channel Inquiry Quotient (CIQ)**. The *Mind* constantly fills in blanks, builds bridges, and completes puzzles, even when the pieces don't belong to you. This capacity is a beautiful, inherent ability. As you become more aware of the production while it unfolds, you can recognize how past impressions influence what you perceive.

Mind is often associated with just thought, but its greatest gift lies in shaping meaning. It is the cognitive processor of experience, attributing, hypothesizing cause and effect, and co-creating the internal architecture of experience. Your moment-to-moment ability to notice, question, and re-author the stories you tell yourself is your CIQ. It represents not traditional intelligence, but rather your living ability to explore, interpret, and reshape the stories you're telling yourself in real time—as the fluid, adaptive quality of the *Mind* in motion: How you organize meaning, notice patterns, reframe narratives, and ask the next question.

Just as I distinguished between *Body*, brain, and *Mind*, the *Mind*, as we explore it here, is the living, interpretive field through which thoughts are shaped and perspectives are formed. Refining your CIQ allows you to participate more consciously in that framing. The *Mind* shifts from dominating the experience to collaborating with the other channels. It listens to the *Body's* cues before inventing a reason. An agile CIQ stabilizes attention and allows meaning to emerge from presence rather than assumption or only recalling and replicating past interpretations. It supports *Spirit*'s clarity by reducing narrative noise. CIQ matures across the 4-S process—from noticing inherited narratives (**Discovery**), to practicing reframes (**Development**), to sustaining clarity under pressure (**Mastery**), to recognizing Mind as a tool rather than an identity (**Knowledge**).

Practices for Strengthening CIQ (Narrative Inquiry)
Strengthening your CIQ is less about controlling thought and more about becoming intentional with how it's structured. These are ways of listening differently.

- **Focused Attention Training:** Return to a single task with full presence. When the *Mind* wanders, notice it and gently guide attention back (*Spirit* sets the focus; *Mind* learns to cooperate).
- **Narrative Re-authoring:** Notice a recurring self-story, such as "I'm always wrong" or "I'm always right." Ask: "Who wrote this version? What else could be true?"

- **Mental Mapping:** Sketch out your thought process. Visualize how one belief connects to another to see the hidden architecture.
- **Reflection through Journaling:** Write without editing. Let your thoughts reveal the patterns they usually hide.
- **Cognitive Pauses:** When you feel stuck in a loop, pause and ask: "What question am I living inside of right now?"

You don't need a retreat as the only option to deepen your CIQ. You just need to create space between perception and interpretation. A few micro-checks can reshape your experience in real time:

- **Pause and Rename:** Is this emotion *worry*, or is it *anticipation*? Is this thought a *judgment*, or is it *discernment*?
- **Follow the Thread:** Where did this story begin? "Am I reacting to this moment, or to a memory of another one?"
- **Try the Angle Shift:** What happens if you test a benevolent hypothesis about the other person's intent?

The *Mind* is one of consciousness's most brilliant tools. It remembers, organizes, and imagines. When the CIQ is refined, we gain more than understanding; we gain access to clarity, redefinition, and new experience. You do not have to silence the mind to live freely. You only have to notice how it shapes the moment you're living and invite it to do so with curiosity, not certainty. In that spaciousness, the *Mind* becomes less of a judge and more of a guide, and inquiry becomes a path toward coherence. With a refined CIQ, the *Mind* shifts from soloist to arranger—placing the *Body's* tones and the *Heart's* overtones into a score that Spirit can conduct.

But meaning is not just constructed in thought; it is also felt. Our journey now takes us from the cognitive to the resonant, from the narrative architect to the feeling conductor. We turn now to explore the third channel: the *Heart*.

Heart | Emotional Resonator

For many years, I interacted with people who longed for peace, often guarded by the idea of love as a deity, a force, or an emotion. Some justified anger as a form of zeal born from love. Others equated love with obedience or moral judgment. Still others professed love for a person one day, only to express hatred or resentment toward them the next. These emotional contradictions appear throughout human history, across all cultures. We'll later revisit *Love* in Chapter 15 as more than a mood or rule.

This raises important questions. Is *love* an emotion, a force, a state of being, or a morally grounded decision? Are emotions triggered by thoughts, or are thoughts triggered by emotions? How do we differentiate a feeling from a physical sensation, or from a meaning we attribute to something external? These questions point us toward a key idea: *Emotion* as the ongoing field of resonance in our *Heart* channel, shaped by an interplay with our thoughts, physical sensations, memory, and intention.

We often speak of emotion as something we feel, but let's also consider it as something we live through. Emotions influence how we hear, respond, and remember. They influence our decisions, relationships, and even how we breathe. They imprint themselves on every layer of experience. I once knew someone whose inner landscape was marked by persistent anger. It didn't seem to matter whether we were discussing politics, the past, or where to place a glass of water—his emotional tone rarely shifted. Anger, it seemed, colored his interpretation of others, shaped his memory of events, and affected his choices. Over time, the emotion became part of how experience was lived and how identity was formed. In situations where kindness, contentment, or a sense of being cared for are present, the body becomes less tense, breathing becomes calmer, and one can be more present and aware. Emotional tone doesn't stay in the background; it influences how the moment takes shape.

Often, emotions are boxed in as "being emotional," a sign of weakness or distraction, or a sign of honesty, candidness, and sincerity. But *resonance* isn't about mere identity, strategy, or openness. The *Mind* may interpret, and that interpretation may clash head-on with a preferred persona or an identity others rush to project or one you have adopted for a long time. Consider emotion as the felt tone of alignment—the *amplification* of *consonance* or *dissonance* your system registers before the mind labels it; the labels are stories about the tone; the tone is the data.

Emotions aren't binary good/bad. They live across ranges: valence (pleasant to unpleasant), activation (calm to agitated), orientation (approach to avoidance), and depth (fleeting to enduring). Resonance amplifies and signals coherence; dissonance signals useful mismatch—and both can be catalysts for awareness.

> ***Note:*** *In music and physics, consonance and dissonance are true opposites: harmonious stability versus tension or clash. Resonance, however, is not the opposite of dissonance. It describes an amplifying effect—how two frequencies, whether consonant or dissonant, reinforce each other's vibration when aligned. Consonance and dissonance describe the quality of the relationship between frequencies. Resonance describes the magnitude of vibration when frequencies align.*
>
> *In this book, when I speak of resonance or dissonance, I am naming the felt polarity of lived experience: Resonance is coherence, alignment, and expansion. Consonance is a match, an expansion, or a "fit." Dissonance is a mismatch, a contraction, or a "misfit." This experiential use is not about musical theory but about the Heart channel's way of registering emotional tone before the Mind labels it. Resonance, consonance, and dissonance are valuable: each signals how experience is aligning (or misaligning) with your system, your intent, and your environment.*

The *Heart Channel of Experience* refers to an energetic channel that receives and resonates with emotional frequencies, distinct from the physical organ or a simple poetic metaphor. In the Flow of Existence, the *Heart* is the resonant register the *Faculties* (Stage 4) tune through, not the filter itself; it is shaped by *Perspective* (Stage 5) and steered by *Spirit (attention + intention)*. Labels arise in *Perspective* and are selected by *Attention's* collapse. *Emotional resonance* is the *Heart* channel's felt measure of consonance or dissonance between what is happening and your system's current patterns internally (needs, values, expectations, memories, boundaries), externally (the situation, other people's signals, context), and your intent (intended outcome), all prior to conceptual labels. Consonance doesn't mean "right," and dissonance doesn't mean "wrong"—each is a signal about fit.

There is a well-established field of research around Emotional Intelligence—its importance in leadership, mental well-being, relational skills, and behavioral flexibility. This section builds on that foundation while offering a complementary lens. **Channel Empathy Quotient (CEQ)** is your ongoing capacity to recognize emotional tone (consonance/dissonance) in yourself and others, and to attune without being swept away. The *Heart* doesn't ask for definitions; it responds to tone and presence. Whereas the *Mind* organizes meaning, the *Heart* shapes the *quality* of that meaning.

CEQ matters because it offers a deeper signal for how you're relating to the present. With a refined CEQ, you don't simply "have emotions"; you engage with them as meaningful data. This doesn't mean dramatizing every feeling, but recognizing its presence and interpreting how it is influencing your view. When your CEQ is refined, it harmonizes with the other channels. The *Body* supplies activation (pulse, breath, tension), the *Mind* supplies appraisal and the label later, the *Heart* detects harmonics across those signals (consonance/dissonance; expansion/contraction; warmth/coolness), and *Spirit (attention + intention)* sets *what* gets amplified and *why* (bandwidth & aim). CEQ creates space for emotion to inform without dominating.

Practices for Refining CEQ (Emotional Attunement)

CEQ is deepened by presence and attention. These practices encourage resonance without overwhelm, supporting clarity rather than restriction.

- **Emotional Labeling:** Consider that you may race to label an emotion based on past experiences or adopted beliefs. While giving an emotion a name when it arises (e.g. sad, happy, angry) may be helpful, remember your positioning within the spectrum of Polarity, where it is not either/or.
- **Breath & Emotion Tracking:** Notice how your breath changes with different emotions. Begin to associate emotional tone with physical rhythm.

- **Relational Check-ins:** Practice attuning to others' emotional shifts in low-stakes moments without trying to label, fix, or manage them.
- **Expressive Resonance:** Draw, move, or write from an emotional place. Let feelings have a channel that doesn't require intellectual explanation.
- **Compassion Practices:** Offer warmth inward, especially when an emotion is hard to interpret. This builds capacity without requiring resolution.

Once you have some practice, you can use these micro-checks to recalibrate at any moment:

- **Feel Tone:** Pause and ask: "What's the emotional tone of this moment?" "Is there tension, tenderness, boredom, or openness?"
- **Optional Light Label:** Identify one dominant emotion. Observe how it is influencing your words, posture, or tone.
- **Feel into the Edges:** Ask: "Where does this emotion live in my body?" "What is it asking for right now?"

These small reflections increase emotional coherence and self-trust. Emotion is part of how we know the moment; it gives color to thought and resonance to presence. Tuning your CEQ doesn't require you to feel everything deeply or to pinpoint a specific label. It asks only that you remain aware of emotional tone as a dynamic participant in your experience.

When we relate to emotion as a channel of experience, we open new pathways to understanding ourselves. But what directs this flow of sensation, thought, and feeling? This leads us to the final channel—the one that orients all the others. We now turn to explore the nature of *Spirit (attention + intention)*.

Spirit (Attention + Intention) | The Guiding Compass

They say a horse knows the truth of a person before the person knows it themselves. It was a crisp morning on the plateau. A man stood beside a large, patient horse. He was well-prepared: clear goal, steady hand, years of training. He intended to lead the horse to the stream below. But the horse wouldn't move. The man repeated the command firmly. Still, the horse stood still. An old trainer nearby watched quietly, then walked over and said, "There are two riders on that horse—one seen, one hidden. The horse obeys the stronger one."

The man froze in recognition. He'd shown up with a clear intention, but underneath his calm exterior was a subtle tension—a need to prove himself, a fear of being judged. The horse had picked up on that deeper current, the hidden one. It wasn't resisting; it was responding. Just like that, something shifted in the man. His shoulders dropped. His breath deepened. He simply stood still, allowing all the unseen riders within him to come into view. Only then did the horse begin to walk.

During a time of my own self-discovery and research, I participated in a series of sessions with a coach, a close childhood friend, who facilitates self-discovery through guided interactions with horses. The horses were not trained to follow commands during these interactions; they were brought in just to *be*. They responded to presence. No masks held. No tactics worked. What you brought, they reflected. They mirrored back internal states—discomfort, congruence, resistance, sincerity.

One core exercise was to lead a horse to the center of a ring without touching it, bribing it, or using props. One participant focused on his excuses and how he suddenly didn't feel well. The altitude, he said, made it too hard for him to concentrate; the horse didn't move. Another grew frustrated, scoffing that the task was a waste of time to mask her fear of failure or lack of control. Her attention was on how others might see her inability to lead; the horse remained still. A third one simply stood, closed his eyes, and focused on *feeling* his intent on connecting with the horse; when he opened them and walked, the horse followed. One participant simply stood, silent tears tracing her face. No explanation. Her attention scattered through emotion, thought, and vulnerability; the horse moved closer to her and remained by her side—neither one moving. The last participant approached with calm curiosity. At one point, she softly asked the facilitators if she could use a harness. It was against the initial directive, but they nodded. She returned, made contact, and together walked to the center. Each person revealed where their attention and intention were aimed.

None of these were right or wrong, correct or incorrect. No one failed because the actual task was for each one to learn from their inner state, not simply to move the horse. But the contrast revealed something vital: same situation, same conditions, different expressions of attention and intention. Through observation, the analysis provided by the coach and his psychologist partner, and subsequent conversations with each participant, it seemed clear: one masked shame and intent through excuse, one redirected attention through defiance, one found resonance, consonance and trust, one exposed raw vulnerability, and one adjusted with pragmatism and adaptedness. I realized that even in the wildest currents, through our *Spirit Channel of Experience*—where we place *attention* and set *intention*—becomes the rudder steering every ripple of experience.

Your *tuning/attuning* capacity for clear focus and coherent intent is your **Channel Alignment Quotient (CAQ)**. CAQ isn't about never being distracted; it's about swiftly realigning when your attention drifts. Where the other channels respond to input, CAQ plays an active role in guiding what we engage, how we prioritize, and where we place our energy. In the Flow of Existence, *Intention* sets the vector (Stage 3), while *Attention* selects and stabilizes the focus (Stage 5). CAQ is the competency that keeps those two in phase. A single moment can be scattered or clear, reactive or focused, depending on how our attention is participating. When CAQ is strengthened, the *Body* responds with steadier breath, the *Mind* interprets with less narrative noise, and the *Heart* resonates with more clarity. CAQ gives experience a steering function and reduces drift, pointing awareness where it is most needed.

Practices for Aligning CAQ (Attention + Intention)

Cultivate your CAQ with simple practices that sharpen focus and clarify intention.

- **Morning Intention Ritual:** Begin the day by naming one quality to live through (e.g. patience, focus, openness).

- **Attention Reset:** When you notice distraction, pause and ask: "Where is my attention? Is it where I want it to be?"
- **Single-Task Focus:** Practice full presence in one small activity—brushing your teeth, writing a message, walking.
- **Values Review:** Periodically reflect on your lived values or priorities. Are your actions aligned with them?
- **Anchor Word Practice:** Choose one word for the week (e.g., integrity, ease) and use it as a guide.
- **Single-point collapse:** For 20 seconds, choose one sensory anchor and hold it without switching.

You can also use these micro-calibrations to realign in any moment:

- *Where is my focus now?*
- *What was my original intention?*
- *Has context shifted, and have I adjusted my attention with it?*
- *What would alignment feel like right now—in my Body, Mind, and Heart?*

Attention and *intention* determine the rhythm and direction of experience. When they are aligned, we live with presence and act with clear intent. CAQ supports this integration as a steady return to clarity. This is the function of *Spirit* as a channel: to bring awareness into motion and to guide experience with *intention* and *attention* working in harmony.

Weaving the Foundations of Awareness into the Channels

The *Four Channels of Experience* are where life becomes tangible—where sensations arise, thoughts form, emotions resonate, and intention directs our focus. Each one is continuously influenced by the deeper structures we have explored.

The foundational models we've explored are not sequential steps but ever-active forces that inform and tune how experience is configured through the four channels in any given moment. They are pillars that define the quality of our awareness:

- **Words Do Matter:** The language and questions you choose create the grammar of your experience.
- **I Am:** The ever-present anchor of awareness beyond persona—the experiencer.
- **Duality/Polarity:** The spectrum of possibility that opens when you move from "either/or" to "both/and."
- **Perception, Viewpoint, and Perspective:** The framing (positional + interpretive) lens that defines what you see and what you believe is possible.
- **Belief, Faith, Conviction, and Knowledge:** The inner energetic posture that tunes your intention and attention.

These foundations are not background theory; they shape every breath, word, and insight. The *Body*, *Mind*, *Heart*, and *Spirit* are where the groundwork becomes lived—where foundations show up as felt, expressed, and directed experience. The map below illustrates how each foundational model continuously informs the *Four Channels*—showing not abstractions, but the very texture of how awareness configures experience.

Model ↓ \ Channel →	Body	Mind	Heart	Spirit (attention + intention)
Words Do Matter	Names or neglects bodily signals	Scripts inner dialogue	Names emotional tone	Frames what we focus on
I Am	Grounded or reactive presence	Observes thoughts	Witnesses emotions or fuses with them	Anchors attention in self-presence
Duality/ Polarity	Release to Tension spectrum	Holding paradox (both/and)	Full emotional spectrum	Deliberate aim to default drift
Perception, Viewpoint, & Perspective	Felt safety or threat	Zoomed-in or zoomed-out lens	Empathy or judgment filter	Inside-out or outside-in focus
Belief, Faith, Conviction, & Knowledge	Trusts or ignores body signals	Rigid conviction or flexible inquiry	Open or closed resonance	Aligned intention or scattered focus

Quick map: I Am = origin of agency; Spirit = aim (attention + intention); Faculties tune the field; Channels shape experience.

When these models are active and aligned, the Four Channels cohere. Experience stops feeling like something that "happens to us" and starts revealing how we are actively shaping and interpreting what we live. The *Body* reflects a felt connection to presence. The *Mind* generates stories rooted in lived meaning. The *Heart* resonates with insight, and the *Spirit* focuses through clear intention. In harmony, these channels reflect the clarity and coherence of the underlying foundations.

We have journeyed through the very architecture of experience, from the raw data of our senses to the stories we tell ourselves. We have seen how the four channels—*Body*, *Mind*, *Heart*, and *Spirit (attention + intention)*—are not empty vessels but living shapers of experience, continuously tuned by our language, our sense of *I Am*, our relationship with polarity, our frame of perception, and the nature of our beliefs. With this integrated map in hand, we now turn to *Who* is living through it all—not just channels and foundations, but the multi-faceted being they serve: *Faceted BEing*.

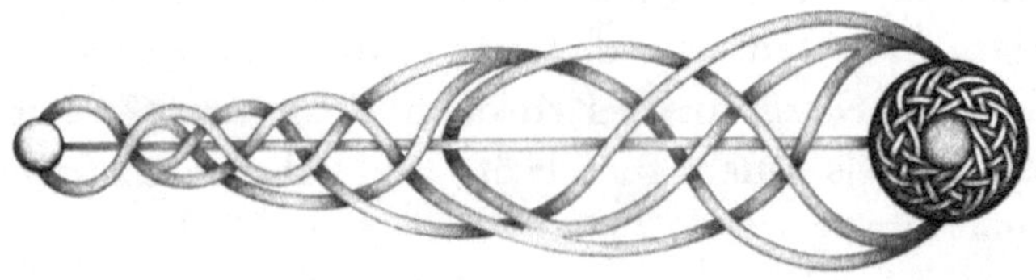

CHAPTER NINE

Faceted BEing

Outward, Mirror, Inward, Authentic Self

There was no single moment when the unmooring began. It was gradual, layered; a thousand key ruptures in a structure I had spent nearly thirty years holding up. For most of my adult life, I experienced the path of a dedicated and passionate minister; it was not just what I did—it was who I thought I was. A soul intending to serve humbly and effectively through a given mandate. But at some point, the ground trembled, and the foundations I believed were unshakeable—suddenly felt unsteady. As doctrines shifted, interpretations revised, and narratives edited and rebranded as fresh revelations, new insights, or greater understandings, I also asked new questions, not out of defiance, but from a place of honest inquiry. These shifts made sense within a large, evolving organization, but the same occurred within me: a deeper, inner misalignment I didn't understand.

The unseen triggers were next: a perception of betrayal and abandonment. The kind that detonates something inside you that was once alive but buried deep inside: a sense of loneliness, fear of disappointing others, and a desperate urge to run somewhere far away. Soon after, the realization that much of what I had been defending, I no longer fully believed about myself or the ability to convey a convincing message. Something in me was no longer willing to perform alignment where there was none.

After deciding I couldn't continue, I finally resigned. It wasn't a decision; I fell apart. My system couldn't keep up with the weight of a persona it didn't have the energy to animate anymore. What followed was not freedom, not right away. What followed was grief and a depression so deep it whispered, *you have no value without the role*. I hadn't just resigned a position. I had lost the reflection that told me I mattered—the social mirror that once said, *you are useful, you are right, you are good*. That mirror shattered. When it did, I couldn't tell if there was anything left behind it.

I searched for that *me*, the one who had once stood with conviction. But I couldn't find him anymore. I wondered—had he ever really been there? Or had I just become a story others believed, and one I felt obligated to keep living? And then came the guilt and shame. Not just for resigning, but for having inspired others to remain within a framework I had so fervently believed in, and now I wasn't in it.

For so many years, I had distanced myself from family—from friendships that couldn't fit inside the framework. I believed I was sacrificing for a higher purpose. But now, I wasn't sure I even understood what purpose meant. When all that cracked open—when marriage, ministry, and meaning all slipped through my hands—I did what many do in absence of clarity: I reached for a new identity. Just another mask, another structure to stand in.

I found comfort in what never reciprocates—attachments that only wanted to squeeze life out of me for their own survival. I found company in confusion, in choices that made no sense, in restless searching for meaning in places that reflected only distortion back. I hid behind shame and guilt, made poor choices, and pushed people away. All while asking myself: if I am not that role, that reflection, that story... then what am I? Life didn't seem worth it anymore, and knocking on the door to the other side appeared like the only way.

When the mask falls, what remains is not a role, but the one who watches.

Through all of this, something remained. Something beneath the collapse that didn't collapse. Something that never needed a role or a title to exist. The *I AM*, witnessing, observing the performance and granting unconditionally. It's like wandering through a house of mirrors: some show you taller, others shorter, some distort your shape beyond recognition. The *Outward* mask smiles because it's trained to. The *Mirror* projects the reflection others want to see. The *Inward* self searches for truth in the fog. But behind one of those mirrors is a pane of clear glass. And through it, if you stop long enough, you notice *who* has been watching all along. Not judging, not performing, just present.

Looking back, I don't regret the service or the love I shared. What I realized is that I forgot about myself. That starting within is key. That although I gave unconditionally and wholeheartedly, I didn't do so to myself. I realized how easily we mistake the costume for the being inside it, how subtly identity becomes entangled with a sense of duty, and how the deeper truth of who we are gets buried beneath a thousand expectations.

The Illusion of Self

In times of confusion, when feeling lost, we may try to *find* ourselves—or one we would hope to be—as if there is one hidden version waiting to be found. But what if the sense of self that is defended, described, or attempted to be fixed is not a single unit but more of a composite? Much of what is referred to as "self" is assembled—layered through memory, language, social reflection, and emotional habit. It feels real because it's familiar, but it is a story in motion.

When the roles we've relied on no longer hold, and the stories we've told ourselves stop making sense, what remains is often depression, disorientation, emptiness, and the question: If I am not the role I invested in for so long, then who am I?

From a young age, we learn to answer the question "Who are you?" with labels: a name, a role, a personality type. These responses become the building blocks of our self-image. We are praised for being a certain way or criticized for not being something else. We internalize preferences, fears, and defense patterns, then start to behave in alignment with them because they are familiar paths or they give us a sense of belonging. Someone calls you generous and you may begin to act more generously. Someone labels you as difficult, and you may defend or conform. But the label entered your field—it became part of what you respond to. Even resistance may become a kind of agreement: "I will define myself in contrast to what they expect." Either way, the mirror has shaped the self. Your language may reinforce this. Statements like, "I've always been the strong one," or "That's just who I am," are lived architecture.

As we've explored, a deeply held belief constructs the self. Identity also organizes around opposites—introverted or extroverted, sensitive or insensitive. These poles offer contrast, but they can also narrow your range of choice unless you remember you exist on a spectrum, capable of experiencing both confidence and uncertainty.

One of the most persistent illusions is believing that you are a fixed identity that never changes. This sense of continuity may feel safe, but if you pay close attention, you'll see that personality and identity aren't constant. The sense of self is malleable. What always remains is not a story; it's the awareness that experiences it. The *I Am*.

Disorientation, uncomfortable as it is, can be a gift. It's a sign that the identity built has reached its limits and something more aligned is ready to be experienced, allowing space for authentic expression. In many spaces, authenticity is promoted as a call to be seen as *different*. But this often becomes another performance, where you measure your originality against someone else's. I once had a conversation with a cousin who believed that people who wore branded clothing were inauthentic and just conforming. What she may not have realized was that her own fashion—styled to be intentionally different—was part of a widely shared "no-style" style. *Authenticity*, in this work, is not about uniqueness as distinction from others. It is about alignment: the degree to which your thoughts, choices, and expressions arise from your own living awareness, not from the need to prove or stand apart.

A very powerful realization is this: **Not only are you intrinsically free to express, you already do.** That freedom can be forgotten, influenced, or suppressed, but it cannot be revoked. That kind of freedom carries responsibility. Not just to avoid harm, but to recognize that you are the one who shapes your experience. You are free to believe something new, to reframe how you think, and to choose how you live that freedom. Even when you feel confused or unsure, something in you is still choosing. That something—the presence behind the pattern—is where your authenticity lives.

Chapter 4: I Am names the presence beneath every role; *Faceted BEing* shows how that presence is filtered and expressed. It reveals four dimensions of self we continuously live through: *Outward*, *Mirror*, *Inward*, and *Authentic*. Each one shapes how we participate in life and how we are perceived—by others and by ourselves.

Four Facets of BEing

Who else can truly know you, if not you?

You may have heard someone tell you or someone else, "I know you better than you know yourself." But is that possible? Sure, they may identify your patterns or predict your reactions, but they cannot truly *know* your inner world. Not your thoughts as they arise, your emotional textures as they swell, or your intent before it finds words. At best, others see your behavior. Only *you* can sense the intent behind it.

Even *we* often lose sight of *ourselves*. We learn to perform, adapt, please, and protect. We become actors in our own story, playing roles that family, culture, and religion handed down, shaping the *Outward* self to resemble what we hope will be loved or accepted. But pretending is not the same as being. Pretending is a performance driven by fear or longing. *Being*—worthily, authentically, and freely—is led by expanded awareness.

We are perhaps the only species uneasy with simply *being*. We think we must earn love, prove worth, and craft meaning. Yet the spark of authenticity always remains beneath the performance, the patterns, and the perception. You are not necessarily what others see. You are not even what you may have seen through conditioned filters. You are the one who can choose to see clearly.

You don't experience life as one identity; you live through many. You may project one version of yourself, receive reflections from others, and interpret what feels real beneath it all. These aren't contradictions. They're facets. The *Faceted BEing Model* helps you see these dimensions clearly:

- **Outward**: The roles and personas you perform.
- **Mirror**: The images and judgments reflected by others.
- **Inward**: The beliefs and self-talk you carry.
- **Authentic**: The unconditioned sense of self behind every mask.

The aim is not necessarily to merge them into one, but to move with awareness across each, and return, again and again, to what truly aligns.

Outward: Persona and the Performance of Self

After resigning as a minister, the first thing I tried to recover was the minister. Not the title, but the version of myself I had grown comfortable with—the one that *knew* how to walk into a room and belong. The one equipped to find hope and clarity. The one vested in purpose. But *purpose* had become my mask, and the moment it cracked, I didn't know who was left behind it.

Don't get me wrong, through the embodiment of that persona I was privileged to witness beautiful expressions of love, compassion, and hope. A people with an overall willingness to take part in a co-created narrative, scripted from sacrifice, suffering, joy, despair, endurance, fear, faith, dependence, and kindness, constantly reaching in to locate the endless supply of strength and determination to survive the relentless pounding from a force dedicated to dominate a world they feel they don't belong to, trusting and longing for the promise of an assured better world. A phenomenal human exercise of creative power.

Even as I beheld such impressive expressions, the sense that something was still missing kept knocking at the door. So, I did what I thought would help: seek wisdom outwardly in places I hadn't looked. I signed up for therapy at a center that integrated everything from psychology to world religions and from quantum theory to bioenergetics. I told myself I was opening my mind, but in truth, I was trying to rewrite a version of myself that felt whole again. Later I dove into spiritual texts, esoteric knowledge, ancient stories, psychology, philosophy, metaphysics, science, and self-help literature. I took courses, consulted oracles, and sought clarity through shamanic practices and Akashic readings. Ceremony after ceremony, reading after reading. All different, but eerily similar. I was told where I came from, what my divine mission was. And yet, something always felt just out of reach. Was it a search for truth, or for a purpose convincing enough to wear as a new costume? I kept trying on new identity outfits, styling them with intentional precision, albeit still sincerely hoping to find answers.

That's the thing about persona: it doesn't always show up as a performance to impress. Sometimes it's a performance to protect—to hide the part of you that feels uncertain, unanchored, incomplete, and unworthy of simply existing without a title or a reason, or a need to repair. The tendency is to call it "finding purpose," but often, it's about reinforcing a version of self that needs a reason to be accepted. "If I help others, I am good." "If I make lots of money, I am successful." "If I wear the right mask, I'll be loved."

Notice simple personas maintained with exhausting consistency, identities rehearsed so easily: "I'm Latin, so I'm passionate," "I'm a believer, so I am good," "I'm white, so I can't dance," "I'm a Pisces, so I'm intuitive," "I'm a starseed, so I'm connected," "I'm a professional, so I'm accomplished." Often it is the search for the most acceptable—and most impressive—avatar.

There's something beautiful in the human longing to express itself, be seen, and make sense of experience through chosen form; always dancing with meaning, reaching for a reflection that feels true. But expanding awareness begins with recognizing what you're referencing—what ideas, roles, or beliefs are conditioning your expression.

When you recognize the source, you allow yourself to choose opportunities more freely. Expression becomes an *authentic creation* rather than an expected performance. That *authenticity* might not match what others expect. It might not even match what you once expected of yourself. But that's not failure. That's freedom.

Maybe that's why actors are admired so much. Not just for their talent, but for the permission they seem to have to play characters; to embody emotion, shift roles, and inhabit archetypes. Maybe part of what we're really drawn to is the reminder that *we're playing too*, but long to finally express freely—without apologizing for the costume change.

The *Outward* facet is the most visible expression of who you want others to see. It includes how you speak, behave, dress, and present yourself in different settings. It's responsive, shaped by context—by what the situation seems to require, what you've learned is acceptable, and what you believe will keep you safe, liked, or respected.

Shifting between roles and characters can be beneficial, and this doesn't automatically imply dishonesty. They reflect your ability to relate, to read the environment, and to engage with others effectively. So *Outward* is not inherently false. It is *functional*. We need it to participate in society, to communicate, to express belonging. But *Outward* is always partial: it is what we *show*, not the whole of who we are. The illusion begins when you confuse this projection with *who* you truly are, or rely on it so fully that you lose awareness of what's happening within.

The friction begins when the *persona* outlives its purpose or is mistaken for the essence. We may polish it endlessly, adjusting it to meet expectations, but the risk is mistaking the surface for the substance. *Outward* is the interface, not the essence. A *persona* repeated often enough becomes a self-expectation. When that expectation doesn't align with your inner truth and potential, it creates strain.

Persona isn't the problem—it's mistaking the mask for the whole that fractures authenticity.

This adapted self may not always reflect what you truly value. The key question becomes: *Is this expression aligned, or just rehearsed?* When your outward expression becomes a mask that hides—when the behaviors you present are not reflecting a current truth but a version of yourself you must maintain—you feel an inner disconnection, and exhaustion introduces itself. The more we over-identify with the *persona*, the harder it becomes to access authentic thought, emotion, full potential, and choice. The mask becomes a full performance—an identity held together by approval, status, or habit.

The *Outward* self is not meant to be erased; it is meant to be re-tuned—realigned with the awareness that designs it. Alignment happens when your outward expression reflects the *observing self* without filters, the presence behind all stories and roles. Expression becomes less about proving or hiding, and more about participating—authentically and intentionally—in the unfolding moment as it manifests. What you show becomes congruent with what you genuinely wish to experience. The outcome of the expression, the manifestation, is *always your own design*, so let it occur from a clear and conscious choice, from truth and the full range of expression; where the outfit, the styling, the material, and the colors match the uninhibited designer.

Awareness Practice: Observing the Outward Self

Realignment begins with noticing how we are showing up in real time. The Outward self can be a valuable entry point for self-awareness when we observe it across all four experiential channels. Focus on the effort to maintain the mask regardless of who is watching.

- **Body:** "Where do I hold tension to maintain this image?" "Is my posture relaxed, or am I physically 'holding up' an image?"

- **Mind:** "What script am I following right now?" "Am I speaking from my center, or reciting what I think 'someone like me' should say?"
- **Heart:** "Am I projecting certainty to hide confusion?" "What vulnerability am I actively shielding?"
- **Spirit (attention + intention):** "Is my intent to connect, or to control how I am perceived?" "Am I anchored in authenticity, or just broadcasting a signal?"

These simple inquiries reopen the dialogue between projection and presence. Over time, your *Outward* facet (persona) softens into a responsive instrument—one that moves in harmony with your inner world rather than overshadowing it. But no facet exists in a vacuum; it is always reflected back to us.

Mirror (Social Reflection)

You are never seen in isolation. Every word you speak, every gesture you make, is perceived by others and reflected back, sometimes with clarity, sometimes with distortion. From early childhood onward, we begin to form a sense of self not only by how we feel inside, but by how we are mirrored by those around us. Are we encouraged, dismissed, praised, or misunderstood? These and other reflected cues accumulate, forming impressions we often mistake for identity. The *Mirror* facet is forged by that dynamic—by others' reflections and the stories we build around them. The issue is not that you are seen, but how easily you may come to believe that what others reflect must be who you are.

Not long after resigning from ministry, I decided to visit the family who had set me on that path all those years ago as a teenager. Their son had captivated me with conversations about God, extraterrestrials, the paranormal, destiny, and other subjects for which I was seeking answers. His father, a wise old man, carried a grounded spiritual presence that impressed me deeply. They introduced me to a belief system that filled my once-aimless world with meaning. Now, thirty years later, I returned—not as the lost teenager, but as someone unraveling and questioning. I didn't go seeking answers, but I did hope for connection, perhaps even inspiration. The grief, however, was still fresh and the depression was still real.

The welcome was warm, almost dazzling. I was treated like a visiting dignitary. Just before dinner was served, I told the wise old man that I had resigned. He received it calmly. But when the family gathered and asked me to lead the prayer—as I still held, in their eyes, the highest ministry—he had to intervene, asking his son to lead the family instead. The shift was immediate. The son became visibly tense. The warmth disappeared, replaced by suspicion. He didn't look at me with openness from then on, but with narrowed eyes, as if trying to decode a hidden agenda. How could I have resigned?! The rest of the evening was tense and defensive.

The next day they invited me to lunch, perhaps to mend what had unraveled. Trying to spark connection, I began to share some of the new ideas that had reignited my inner wonder, the kind of topics we used to revel in. I expected curiosity; I received confrontation.

"Why are you here?" the son asked, his voice sharp and loud. "What are you trying to get from us?" I was stunned. "You didn't come to visit—you're here for something else. What is it you want?" His words sounded angry and accusatory, delivered with the intensity of a man guarding not a home, but a narrative—a version of the past that couldn't stand now that I had stepped outside the role he had once cast me in.

After an even more agitated interaction, I stood up, calm but firm, and left the house. I didn't ask for a ride or expect to be stopped. I walked for miles alone, through unknown roads, in a country I barely knew. The ground beneath me felt unsteady, but my steps did not. As I walked, I didn't feel heroic or righteous. I felt awake. The pain and disappointment were real, but something else had clicked into place. I had walked out because everything in me knew I didn't belong there anymore—not as they saw me, not as I had once seen myself. The version of me they felt so proud of—the lost teenager who became a minister, the pearl in their crown—had crumbled. To him, without even asking why I had resigned, I had failed. This time, I didn't try to earn back acceptance or explain myself from fragments I no longer recognized. I chose not to contort myself to fit someone else's mirror. That walk was more than a departure; it was a return to myself, even if I couldn't yet name the *Self* I was returning to.

Eventually, I understood that the interaction was a clash with the *Mirror*; a reflection not only of external perception, but of how those views influence your sense of self and the permission you grant yourself to simply *be*. What I saw reflected back was not who I was in that moment, but the lost character from *their* story. A trophy of salvation. A symbol of legacy. A story they had proudly shared. When that story was not intact anymore, my value, through their lens, was revoked. Honestly, I can't pretend to *know* with absolute certainty their inner thoughts or feelings. This was my perception, my experience, from my viewpoint and perspective.

Sometimes the *Mirror* is like a funhouse—distorting us to match another's expectation, making us seem taller, shorter, more of this or less of that. Mirroring is two-way: you interpret others through your narrative, even as they interpret you through theirs. Often, what gets reflected has less to do with *who you are* and more to do with *what others need to see*.

> *The Mirror doesn't show who you are; it shows who others perceive.*

From our earliest moments, identity is formed between our expression and others' reactions. A child laughs, and someone smiles back, reinforcing the value of the expression. A child cries and is shushed, registering what is safe to express. These and many other micro-reflections accumulate into patterns. We associate approval with certain behaviors, discomfort with others, and slowly construct a self-image built from reflected feedback. Labels from family, teachers, and culture—*You're smart, you're difficult, you're the quiet one*—develop a character in the narrative of our inner life. We don't just receive these reflections; we adopt or reject them. This adaptation can be useful, but when it becomes habitual or fear-driven, your *Outward* expression orbits someone else's expectation rather than your own alignment.

Not all reflections are accurate. Some are warped by the beliefs or projections of the person holding the mirror. A parent who equates certain emotions with weakness may mirror back disapproval when expressed. A friend threatened by your confidence may reflect it back as arrogance. Distortion also happens with praise. The "strong one" may suppress vulnerability to keep being seen as stable. The "successful one" may feel unable to ask for help. What started as a reflection becomes an expectation, and eventually a constraint. We may protect the identity others affirmed, and lose sight of the parts of us that weren't invited into the mirror.

Discernment lets you receive others' reflections without letting them define you. It's the ability to pause and ask: "Is this reflection aligned with what I know to be true?" "Is my reaction to this about a past wound?" **Discernment doesn't mean rejecting feedback; it means receiving it with an expanded perspective.** You may still adjust your response to the Mirror, but now you do so from awareness—re-tuning the reflection rather than reacting to it.

Awareness Practice: Engaging the Mirror

By working with the Mirror facet, you recognize when your actions reflect someone else's perception and perspective, and then determine if your reaction is a reflex of defense, or a response aligned with your Authentic Self. Focus on the volatility of self-worth based on external feedback.

- **Body:** "Do I adjust my posture or expression when I sense I'm being watched?" "Am I shrinking to avoid judgment or puffing up for praise?"
- **Mind:** "Who am I trying to please right now?" "Am I editing my words in real-time to match what I think they want?"
- **Heart:** "Why does their silence feel like a threat?" "Am I sourcing my emotional safety from their reaction?" "Is this an echo from past experiences?"
- **Spirit (attention + intention):** "Have I outsourced my authority to them?" "Is my attention on their experience of me, rather than my experience of this moment?"

As you learn to receive reflections without losing your center, the Mirror becomes less a judge and more a guide—redirecting awareness toward the *Inward* facet, where meaning is integrated.

The *Mirror* facet shows how we're seen and our reaction or response to it. Over time, those outer impressions crystallize into inner narratives—beliefs and self-labels we carry about ourselves. In the next section, we turn to the *Inward* facet: the self we believe ourselves to be, and how that internal story continues to shape our experience.

Inward (Self-Perception)

The stories we tell ourselves about who we are don't arrive fully formed; they're stitched together from memory, meaning, emotion, and imagination. The *Inward* facet reveals not only what we believe about ourselves, but how those beliefs are shaped, held, and sometimes protected at all costs. This is the landscape of self-perception: inner narratives assembled from feedback and experience, shaped by upbringing, culture, and belief systems, guarded by secrecy and desire—and reinforced by habit and defenses.

> *Your Inward facet is the story you tell yourself about who you are—fluid when observed, rigid when believed.*

As I mentioned before, during the long search to understand my experience with depression, I explored many paths. A journey driven by both curiosity and an intuition to stop outsourcing truth, leading me down many paths: psychological therapies and energy work; divinatory and metaphysical practices; systemic constellation work and past-life regression; ancestral plant medicines and shamanic ceremonies. Each offered fascinating insights. But one moment stood apart: a guided psilocybin-assisted session, facilitated by a trained indigenous psychologist. It was approached with care, preparation, and deep respect. I entered the session not seeking to affirm a story, but to see clearly; not what I wanted to see, but *what is*.

At first, my mind resisted, clinging to analysis and to structures built up over years. But eventually, a shift in perception—the familiar state I shared about in Chapter 8: "A field of endless peace, love, and serenity where everything made sense." Bear with me as I briefly summarize the visions I experienced for hours, and for now, try to see it as a fantastic movie introduction, regardless of where you stand on *spirituality* and your position on divine attribution.

I envisioned energy patterns, forces and vibrational frequencies, different configurations shaping form, different energetic levels, densities, and realms. Flashes of civilizations in different galaxies, past lives, and connections with other beings. Love in different forms: as a force, a configuration, and as intention itself. I giggled in awe at the majestic composition of imagery. But the giggles were mostly about a simple, clear insight that came not as a voice or a thought, but as a knowing: *It is much simpler than you make it out to be.* I had expected to confront the worst of myself, but there was no such thing. No judgment, no explanation. Just presence, wholeness, and the understanding that all experiences are an act of creation. I realized that the story I had made up and believed about myself was just that... a story. I was my worst judge, and still, my screenwriter, my costume and character designer; whole and capable of redesigning from the inside out.

The Inward facet houses the premises of the stories you've accepted about yourself. Just as you create stories about others through perception, you also construct inner stories about who you are. But perception is not permanent. Similar to how you previously embraced narratives about yourself and who you should be, you may now choose to discard and revise them. This doesn't mean there is no effect to our actions; it means you can choose how you experience life from this moment of realization.

The *Inward* facet is the internal landscape we carry. It's the running narrative beneath decisions, relationships, and emotions. It influences how you respond to success and failure, how you interpret silence or attention, and how you assign meaning to experience. It forms slowly, built from past experiences, internalized messages, and repeated patterns of thought. It's where you store labels and beliefs you've accepted: *I'm the peacemaker. I'm the problem. I'm the reliable one.* These become *filters* through which you interpret yourself.

The inner narrative becomes problematic when it hardens from a fluid story into a fixed identity. For example, a mistake may become: "I always fail," "I never make mistakes," "Someone else caused this," or "Now I don't deserve..." (or "I deserve punishment"). An insecurity becomes: "I am unworthy" or "They shouldn't see what really is going on inside," often forcing stories that protect us from vulnerability by exaggerating competence or control, or giving up and capitulating. In either case, we lose touch with endless possibility and raw potential, and react instead from the identity we may believe we are. Even if your chosen values, moral and belief systems seem opposite to this proposition, redemption, self-compassion, rehabilitation, and opportunity to correct the "mistake" rely on it.

Two core distortions often take root here. The first is the belief that worthiness must be earned. Somewhere along the way, many of us absorb the idea that we are only "good enough" when we succeed or please others. But worthiness is not conditional on action; it is intrinsic to our existence. The belief in unworthiness is one of the most corrosive inner scripts one can carry. Its effects ripple through individuals and societies alike. It leads to self-sabotage before beginning, withdrawal from meaningful connection, and internal resistance to let go of what is no longer useful—even when wished for. We will explore *Worthiness* in more detail in Chapter 13.

The second distortion is the belief that we are not free, that our choices are controlled by circumstances or the past. But inner freedom doesn't mean ignoring reality; it means recognizing that you always retain the capacity to choose how to relate to it. When the *Inward* story says, "I can't," you live as though you truly can't, even if it *is* possible. When it says, "I'm stuck," the way out faints with every utterance. Recall Key 4 in Chapter 1: "*You are so free that you can choose your own constraints or release them.*"

The inner story can feel immovable, but it's a pattern, not a prison. Rewriting it doesn't mean pretending nothing ever hurt you. It doesn't require erasing a memory or forcing a new belief to cover the old one. It begins with recognizing the story you've been carrying and deciding whether it still belongs. This awareness disables fixed scripts and restores authorship.

You may also choose to update your *Verbal Architecture*, which can change your entire emotional posture:

- "I'm a failure" becomes "I felt discouraged, but there is always a way out."
- "I always ruin things" becomes "That didn't go how I wanted, but I can respond differently next time."
- "I don't deserve this" becomes "This feels unfamiliar, and I'm learning how to receive it."

As you observe your inner story, the foundational models we've explored become powerful tools for this rewriting process. *Words Do Matter*, as the language you use forms the grammar of your self-concept. The *I Am* is the stable foundation beneath every shifting self-perception, the authority to rewrite. *Duality and Polarity* opens the space between rigid binaries like worthy/unworthy. *Perception, Viewpoint, and Perspective* allows you to shift the lens and see your story from a new angle. And finally, making your *BFCK* conscious allows new possibilities to emerge. When these frameworks work together, the *Inward* facet softens from a fixed truth into one expression among many—responsive, adaptive, and increasingly aligned.

Awareness Practice: Observing the Inward Self

Observing the *Inward* facet takes time and patience, but it begins with simply noticing. These cues can help illuminate the stories you're living from:

- **Body:** "What physical sensations arise when I recall a version of myself I no longer want to live from?" "Does my body feel constricted when I repeat an inner narrative?"
- **Mind:** "What recurring thoughts define who I believe I am?" "Are these thoughts narrating the present—or replaying the past?" "Is the mental script I'm using helping me understand or limiting what I explore?"
- **Heart:** "What emotions consistently reinforce my inner story?" "Am I giving myself room to feel something new, or do I keep returning to familiar tones—like shame, guilt, or guarded pride?"
- **Spirit (attention + intention):** "Where is my attention: on reaffirming, conforming, or simply witnessing?" "What

intention drives the story I tell myself—self-protection or self-connection?"

These questions invite spaciousness into your inner landscape, so that the story you live from becomes more conscious, flexible, and aligned with your *who* beneath the narrative.

As you rewrite from within, the inner story becomes transparent enough for the *Authentic* facet to shine through—the awareness beyond narrative. In the next section, we turn to the *Authentic Self*—the living awareness that has been there all along.

Authentic Self

The first time I visited the tribes in the Sierra Nevada, every step felt like a prepared revelation. The air was alive—green, dense, humming. Not long into our journey up the mountain, we passed a wide riverbed, more sediment and debris than water, its flow reduced to a trickle. The surrounding plants were dry and layered with dust. But as we ascended, I noticed that the same river was now much fuller, its water clearer, its sound louder. The landscape was greener, wetter, more alive. I asked the lead Mamo why it was so dry below but full up here.

"Down below, Younger Brother removed the rocks," he said calmly. "They crushed them for construction. They cleared the path for recreation." I mentioned heat and evaporation, trying to make sense of it. He just smiled. "No. With the rocks gone, the flow was disrupted. It sinks. It disappears. Without water, there is no life." I went quiet.

The higher we climbed, the denser the vegetation became, but the path also steepened, filled with small stones and uneven rocks. It took full attention to keep moving forward. The path felt like hard work. I joked with the Mamo, "A lot of stones on this path, huh?" "Yes," he replied, with a familiar pause. "Fortunately." I smiled, knowing something was coming. "If there were no stones," he said, "you wouldn't be able to move forward. You'd slide back." There it was. Another sentence that said everything. Suddenly, the stones were beautiful. They weren't in the way; they *were* the way.

Not long after returning to the U.S., I shared this experience in congregations across several states—always with reverence, always moved. The change in the river's flow, and the presence of the stones. How we often treat stones as symbols of obstacles—things to remove so the journey is smoother. But the stones on our path give us the texture and resistance needed to stay upright and advance with intention. Smooth everything, and we lose our grip. They are there to make forward motion *possible;* to not slide back onto old ground.

The rocks mould and aerate the river's current—preventing stagnation, increasing vitality, and nourishing the ecosystems. Remove them, and the current loses its turbulence—the very movement that keeps the water alive. Without that friction, the flow weakens. As the tribes say: *"Without water there is no life."* Recalling a thought from Chapter 4, the river doesn't flow because it searches for a purpose. Its nature is simply to flow—guided by gravity, shaped by terrain, responding to its environment, and life emerges wherever that flow continues, sustained by movement, not by forcing intention—its flow is guided, not gripped.

Likewise, the *Authentic Self* is not driven by a constructed purpose. It doesn't push or strive. It simply is—present, aware, responsive. It is not an ideal we achieve, but the ever-present foundation of *who you are*, unaltered by roles or judgments. It does not stand apart as a *hidden* witness, nor does it suffer as a victim. Instead, it unconditionally receives every thought, feeling, and identity we've gathered. Personas are simply traces of past choices, but the *Authentic Self* is the ground upon which they arise.

Think of *I Am* as the bare fact of your presence—the very first *note* struck when the *nondual ground* of all existence *differentiates* into a unique center of awareness. It's the recognition "I exist," before any story, role, or identity arises. By contrast, your *Authentic Self* is how that core presence shows up in the world once your stories, beliefs, and learned patterns have been stripped away. It's the lived expression of *I Am* through your four channels—*Body, Mind, Heart,* and *Spirit (attention + intention)*—where your focus is not on reacting from conditioning but responding from your deepest knowing.

The *Authentic Self* is not a goal to achieve, an identity to perfect, or a spiritual badge to wear. It is the ongoing presence that underlies every experience. It doesn't change when your mood changes; it doesn't disappear when you are not aware of it; it is not disappointed when your choice seems regrettable. Its strength is in its receptivity; its clarity comes from not being entangled with outcome. It trusts flow. You might experience alignment with it one moment and feel disconnected the next, but the *Authentic Self* doesn't stand apart, and you're never disconnected. Only your awareness of it drifts.

The misalignment or *static* is what happens when you believe you are the roles you play and identity or persona become a sustained act, a projection of a false character built to protect an unmet need. Just as a lie is not a new creation but a distortion of a hidden truth, believing you are a character in a story is an illusion. It isn't about "What is my authentic expression?" but about what's allowed and what's not. It is usually at this point that you feel like you've "lost" who you are, there is an indescribable void, or when dissonance is labeled as justifiable yet uncontrollable emotions. You are not *lost*, just disoriented. There is no void, you are just uncomfortable in the unknown, and the dissonance from your Heart channel is amplifying the misalignment.

Returning to the *Authentic Self* is not about adding something new, but about a shift in recognition. This return is itself a form of feedback—*Stage* 7 of the *Flow of Existence*—each moment of noticing invites a compassionate course-correction back into presence. Each time you return and attune, you deepen presence. This iterative rhythm is the pulse of awareness learning itself—each cycle refining frequency, restoring resonance. Alignment is coherence—a felt sense that who you are and what you express are moving in the same direction. It often emerges in the space left by surrender, when you stop gripping an old narrative.

When acknowledged, your *Authentic Self* partners with the other facets. Your *Outward* expression is congruent. It softens into presence-led expression—not role maintenance. Your *Mirror* doesn't direct your sense of self; you become less reactive to how you're seen. Your *Inward* isn't limited to old beliefs or inherited narratives. It becomes a tool rather than a foundation. As the current of awareness flows from the Authentic Self through these facets, the energy once bound in maintaining appearances is released into presence itself. This is not the rejection of identity; it is the anchoring of a chosen identity in a deeper truth.

The *Authentic Self* doesn't arrive when everything is resolved. It is always here, as true and limitless potential, giving unconditionally. When you release the need to prove, explain, or become—and allow yourself to simply *be*, here, now—the alignment occurs. The stones may still appear. The reflections may still shift. The story may still resurface. But now, you can coexist with the stones and recognize their value; you recognize that the distortions in every mirror are merely interpretations; you decide what you write from this point forward. Most importantly, you recognize where you're living from—and that awareness itself is home.

Awareness Practice: From the Authentic Self

Recognize the free and unfiltered expressions from the Authentic Self through ordinary moments. These touchpoints across the four channels can help.

- **Body:** "Is my movement originating from ease or effort?" "Does my body feel inhabited and grounded, or bracing for impact?"
- **Mind:** "Am I observing these thoughts, or am I lost in them?" "Is this thought serving a script?"
- **Heart:** "Is the emotion arising from connection, or defense?" "Does this emotional tone reflect consonance or dissonant expectation?"
- **Spirit (attention + intention):** "Is my attention on the joy of expression, or the weight of the outcome?" "Is my intention to align with truth, or to manipulate approval?"

You can also sit quietly and ask:

- **What parts of my life still feel like roles I'm performing?** Which masks do I wear most often—and for whom?
- **When do I feel most fully present?** What are the conditions or moments where I feel most like myself?

- **Where do I notice a gap between how I act and how I feel?** Where might I be ignoring my values to maintain peace, image, or approval?
- **Why do I hold back certain words, choices, or emotions that feel real to me?** What am I protecting—and does it still need protection?
- **How do I respond when I notice I've drifted from being real?** What signals appear in my body, mind, or heart when authenticity fades?
- **Who** is aware of all these movements, questions, and reflections?

These are cues for realignment—small openings where you can return to express from *Authenticity.*

> ***Note:*** *The Faceted BEing is not a hierarchy but a living circuit of awareness. Energy emanates from the Authentic Self, filters through Inward meaning, expresses through Outward action, and returns through the Mirror as reflection. Each cycle refines coherence, aligning expression with essence. Through this loop, awareness learns itself—freeing perception from performance, and letting presence flow unbroken through all its forms.*

Living from the unconditioned *Authentic Self* reorients your relationship with your own being. But this inner alignment naturally changes how you see and connect with others. When you stop seeing yourself as a fixed identity to be defended, you also stop seeing others as mere reflections or roles in your own story. This opens the door to a more profound way of relating, one rooted in compassion and shared presence. In the next section, we explore what it means to see through *The Empathetic View.*

The Empathetic View

The first time Mamo Bartolo took me to a clearing atop the Sierra Nevada, I thought it was just another walk. We had spent several days together already, him patiently sharing, me eagerly marveling. On this day, he led me to a clearing nestled between slopes where they grew everything they needed for their immediate survival.

Demarcated areas held purposeful vegetation. The scent was alive with earth and sun.

"This is where we grow what we need," he said, finally speaking. "Food, spices, building material, medicine," waving his arm and pointing as he named each one. I marveled; it truly felt like a gift, this place where everything necessary was provided in one living system, grown with their own hands and gifted by nature. But he seemed almost apologetic. "It's not like where you come from," he said. "This is all we've got." I couldn't help but respond, "This is the same we have. We also have places to acquire tools, to shop for food, to buy what we think we need. The only difference is, you're wealthier." He laughed and asked why. "Because where I come from," I said, "you need lots of money to access those things. If you don't have it, you go without. But *you* grow what you need. And you know how." He just looked out over the land.

Later, I'd learn more about their community, where everyone has a role. When a couple marries, the whole community helps build their home, and the couple's role in the community is defined prior to finalizing marriage. At school, children bring food from their families' harvest, and parents take turns preparing meals for everyone. They weave their own clothes. They raise what they eat. They make what they use. There is a rhythm. A balance. And yet, he thought I came from abundance. I thought he did. We were two people, standing in the same clearing, sharing the same air, and yet what we saw had been shaped by two entirely different paths. Two separate viewpoints. We are not that dissimilar. We all carry stories and form interpretations. Although the costumes differ, the currents underneath are familiar: happiness and sadness, safety and fear, love and loss. To recognize this in another is empathy. To remember that others, just like *me*, are more than what we see—more than their words, roles, or reactions—is to live from the center of our shared humanity.

The Empathetic View is remembering that others are more than what you perceive—just as you are more than what they perceive.

The *Faceted BEing: Outward, Mirror, Inward, Authentic* model lives in everyone. Just as you each navigate your own layers, so does everyone else. What you encounter in another person may be only one facet, often the *Outward* role or a reaction shaped by the *Mirror*. Judging that surface often reveals more about your own lens than about them. You may sense or anticipate someone's behavior, responses, or patterns, but your viewpoint is uniquely yours. Theirs is theirs. You will never fully *know* what lives in someone's *Inward* self-perception—what they're thinking, what they're feeling, or what they've carried. This isn't a call to ignore harmful behavior, but a reminder that behavior is shaped by more than willpower; it is shaped by history, conditioning, and unseen emotion.

Empathy opens us, but without clarity, it can overwhelm. Compassion doesn't mean carrying what isn't yours; it means being able to remain connected while staying rooted in your own presence. This is the balance:

- Compassion says, "I see you're in pain." Entanglement says, "Now I'm in pain, too."
- Compassion says, "I want to understand you." Entanglement says, "I need to make you feel better so I can feel better."

Awareness helps you recognize the difference. You can sense the energetic field that forms between you and another—the shared space of perception—without becoming entangled in their narrative; you're observing the energetic field co-created between two presence points. This means seeing their *Outward* role with no need to play into it, witnessing their *Mirror* without reinforcing a distorted reflection, honoring their Inward story without merging with it, and trusting that their *Authentic Self*, like yours, is intact and expressing unconditionally from pure possibility, even when obscured. Compassion involves being present to another's experience *without abandoning your own*. That is how you may offer empathy that supports healing.

This way of seeing allows us to move from separation to recognition. Just as we are masterful scriptwriters and directors in the stories we tell ourselves, we are also gifted character designers in the stories we build about others. We often describe who someone is, what they must be thinking, what they want or reject—even before we've truly met them. Sometimes based on a sentence. Sometimes based on a look. Sometimes based only on resemblance to someone else. These internal character sketches may feel like insight, but they are often projections—shaped by our own past experiences, unspoken fears, or incomplete reflections. The more we do this, the more we mistake our interpretation for the whole person in front of us.

By expanding awareness, questions shift from "Why are they like that?" to "What might they be carrying?" From "Why are they acting this way toward me?" to "What does this bring up in both of us?" From "How do I get them to change?" to "How can I stay present to what's true in me while seeing what might be true in them?" Recognition doesn't mean dissolving boundaries, but holding them with compassion, understanding that everyone—beneath their behavior—is a being with facets, just like you.

Practice: Applying the Empathetic Lens

Empathy isn't only about understanding others; it's about noticing the lens through which you see them. Each facet becomes an opportunity to pause and ask:

- **Outward:** What role am I assigning to this person? Am I making space for them to express freely, or am I reacting to who I think they should be?
- **Mirror:** How am I shaping what they feel they need to reflect? Is my body language or tone triggering a protective response in them?
- **Inward:** What inner beliefs about people like them might I be projecting? Am I interacting with this person or with a story I've told myself about them?
- **Authentic:** Am I relating to them as a whole being or as a role? Do I recognize their worth and freedom, even when I disagree with them?

This empathetic lens doesn't ask you to diagnose, but to be aware of the field you're co-creating.

Seeing others through an empathetic lens expands awareness from reflection to participation. Empathy becomes movement—awareness meeting awareness. The next step in this exploration is to look at the dynamic interplay between our inner world and our shared reality. We now turn to *The Dance of Shared Experience*.

The Dance of Shared Experience

How Presence Becomes Co-Creation

Every time two people come into contact—each bringing their own body, thoughts, feelings, and focus—a shared field is created. In that field, what's lived is no longer just *yours* or *mine*, but something new we participate in together. This is the *Dance of Shared Experience*. It happens in every interaction, spoken or unspoken. Our channels engage, our attention flows, and our intention meets the other's. From that interplay, a moment emerges, shaped by both, yet belonging to neither alone.

You bring your sensations, thoughts, and emotional tone; so do they. The moment is shaped not just by what each person brings, but by how those elements meet. A gesture is received, a tone of voice calms or agitates, a question opens or closes space. This shared space is fluid, influenced by mood, posture, memory, belief, and attention. It can become resonant or dissonant, stable or volatile, expansive or compressed, depending on how each person participates.

The table below outlines how each channel contributes to this co-creation:

Channel	Your Expression	Their Expression	What Emerges
Body	Posture, movement, proximity	Gesture, touch, pacing	Physical rhythm, tension, or comfort
Mind	Framing, language, curiosity	Story, interpretation, questioning	A shared narrative or meaning

Channel	Your Expression	Their Expression	What Emerges
Heart	Openness, emotional tone	Empathic resonance or protectiveness	A shared emotional field (trust, grief, etc.)
Spirit (attention + intention)	Where you focus and why	Where they focus and what they aim to create	Alignment (amplification) or friction (misalignment)

When two people are aligned, not in opinion but in quality of presence, the moment opens and trust builds. Shared experience evolves through a natural rhythm of **initiation** (when one person's presence and intent establish the opening tone), **resonance** (the other's emotional, physical, or mental response feeds back into the moment), **adjustment** (each person, consciously or unconsciously, shifts attention, emotion, or posture in response), **emergence** (a new shared expression arises: conversation, silence, insight, rupture, repair—a space where multiple *I Am's* converge into something wholly new), and **continuation** (the shared field refines, deepens, or dissipates based on further participation—which is itself a feedback loop underscoring that shared experience is a calibration process). This is *co-creation*, and every interaction we share moves through these rhythms.

In a conversation, you might ask a meaningful question (*Spirit*), they might respond from the heart (*Heart*), offer a new idea (*Mind*), and you both feel the tone of something deeper forming (*Body*), creating a moment neither could have shaped alone. A ritual, a project, a shared pause. When two or more people bring aligned attention and clear intent, something emerges that transcends each individual's input: Emergence, a *third space* that lives between and beyond.

To participate in this shared field in a healthy way requires awareness. Stay rooted in your *Authentic Self's* potential; the more anchored you are, the more clearly you can contribute. Honor your limits and pause if an interaction becomes overwhelming; redirect attention with care. If the field feels volatile, you can help guide it back toward balance. Shared experience deepens only when both parties remain engaged, attuned, and respected.

Every moment we share is a *Living Dance of Experience.* You are not the sole author of what happens, but you are always a participant. Through Body, Mind, Heart, and Spirit (attention + intention), you help shape what lives between you and another. *Co-creation* is the everyday reality of how we live, listen, and connect. And when two people meet in presence—anchored in themselves and attuned to each other—what's created is not just an interaction. It's a *shared field of being.* But every shared moment, though co-created, is ultimately lived through your own awareness.

Feedback and the Four Facets

In the *Flow of Existence, Feedback* is Stage 7—the loop that takes every manifested moment and re-enters our system right after *Creation/Manifestation* (Stage 6), cycling back through our seven *Faculties* (Stage 4) for recalibration.

She said little: just a quick nod, a tilted glance, and a faint smile that didn't quite reach her eyes. But something tightened inside you. You walked away wondering, "Did I say too much?" Hours later, that moment still lingered. Your mind looped the tone of your own voice, the way you paused mid-sentence. "Why did I say it like that?" "I sounded so awkward." "What if she thinks I'm a mess?" Feedback had arrived. Not from her. From you. Echoes of past dialogues and internalized responses glimmered to life. You weren't responding to her expression anymore. You were responding to yourself.

Feedback is more than something we receive; it is the field we continually generate. It echoes through every conversation, silence, and inner commentary. Whether spoken aloud, implied by a glance, or repeated silently in the mind, *feedback* becomes the mirror in which we judge, adjust, or defend who we believe we are. It serves reinforcement as much as improvement. What we echo, we strengthen. What we repeat, we inhabit.

Without awareness, feedback can become a script we follow without question. With awareness, it becomes a tool: a lens for perception, a prompt for presence, and a reflection of intention. In the work of Mosston and Ashworth, they frame feedback in the process of Teaching and Learning and beautifully expand on the implications of using value-based, corrective, neutral, or ambiguous statements, each of which can be internalized as self-feedback[6].

Value Feedback
Value feedback contains a *judgment word*—either positive or negative. These statements express an evaluation, convey a standard, or signal approval or disapproval. The focus is on the *giver's values*, not the receiver's development. When overused, value feedback can encourage *external validation* dependency rather than internal reflection. Examples: "Very *good*," "Not *bad*," "She's such a *nice* girl," "You are a *looser*."

Corrective Feedback
Corrective feedback highlights a *deviation from expectation or task*. It may include an error, a problem, or the needed correction. The focus is on the *error itself*, not the person. When overused, it can shift attention toward mistakes and away from connection or context, which may result in an *obsession with correctness* or *avoiding mistakes*. Examples: "1 + 2 = 4 is incorrect, the answer is 3," "You arrived 15 minutes late," "You spent $500 from your savings," "You said you would not mention it again. You've mentioned it three times."

Neutral Feedback
Neutral feedback offers *non-judgmental* acknowledgment. It simply describes or reports what occurred, without adding approval, disapproval, or correction. The focus is on the *receiver*, allowing them to interpret or assign meaning. Overuse may lead to feelings of *emotional distance or disconnection* if no warmth or affirmation is ever offered. Examples: "She was promoted to Creative Director," "You lost weight," "Correct, that is what he pointed to," "The voters elected him as the president."

Ambiguous Feedback
Ambiguous feedback lacks obvious intention, evaluation, or factual reference. It leaves interpretation (or misinterpretation) open, often without guidance. The focus and meaning are unclear, which can place *undue interpretive burden on the receiver*. When used

6 Mosston and Ashworth, "Role of Feedback."

frequently, it may create confusion, miscommunication, or a false sense of shared understanding. Examples: "I am doing everything in my power to solve this," "Seems like it," "Interesting," "Are you sure you are right?" "Pretty good."

Let's now frame the feedback you provide to yourself through the lenses of such statements, and the four distinct *Facets of BEing*, noting how each Facet corresponds to a phase of the *4-S Process* and a primary (not exclusively) *Channel of Experience*:

- **Outward (Persona)**: Imagined performance feedback. Commonly engages *Self-Discovery* as you notice the story you prefer to believe about yourself. (Primary Channel: *Mind* — Narrative Architect.)
- **Mirror (Social Reflection)**: Feedback received from others. Often catalyzes *Self-Development* as you distinguish *Authenticity* from projection. (Primary Channel: *Heart* — Emotional Resonator.)
- **Inward (Self-Perception)**: Feedback you give yourself (inner speech) based on what you believe about yourself. Tends to catalyze *Self-Mastery* as you refine the inner loop. (Primary Channel: *Mind*; coupled readout in *Body*.)
- **Authentic Self**: Guidance arising from core self-presence. Deepens *Self-Knowledge*. (Primary Channel: *Spirit (attention + intention)*; recognized across all channels.)

Facet 1: Outward Expression

Feedback in this facet often revolves around performance and a post-analysis of how we imagine we came across. This inner monologue often falls into one of four categories.

Value-Based Feedback

These are judgments that stem from internalized standards, often inherited from the cultural or professional roles you've taken on. They reflect how you want to color the perception you have of yourself. For example: "I nailed it! That was so good. They must have loved it!" or "I should have stayed quiet. I'm awful."

Corrective Feedback
This feedback focuses on a perceived error without necessarily passing harsh judgment. Yet when internalized without compassion, even this can compound insecurity. Here are two ways you can approach when making a mistake: "1 + 2 is not 4. It is 3. I'll correct it," or "1 + 2 is not 4. I always make a mistake."

Neutral Feedback
This feedback observes and describes without obvious approval or disapproval. But even facts, depending on our state of mind, can feel affirming or discouraging. For example: "I am aware I don't understand what they said. There is something I haven't realized," or "I don't always understand others."

Ambiguous Feedback
This kind of feedback lingers and invites interpretation, which is often shaped by our past experiences or insecurities. When clarity is absent, our minds tend to fill in the blanks. For example: *"Interesting approach,"* or *"It is what it is."*

Facet 2: Mirrored Expression of Others
There's a kind of feedback that comes from how we are seen by others. The *Mirror* of others reflects not just our actions, but the meanings, filters, and expectations projected onto them. It also involves projecting others' values onto yourself and making dispositional attributions about their feedback.

Value-Based Feedback
This occurs when someone else's judgment or values are *reflected back at you*. You share an idea and someone says, "Oh, that's wrong." They might intend pointing out an error, but you hear judgment. Notice how, although not objective truth, it's being filtered through your Perspective so it arrives laden with meaning you may or may not own. It may hit you physically (Body), spin into self-talk (Mind), stir an emotional charge (Heart), and scatter your attention and intention (Spirit). The impact of their value-based feedback can linger long after the moment passes because it speaks to core moral and identity schemas, activating deeper emotional and cognitive networks linked to self-esteem and social belonging.

Corrective Feedback
Someone may interrupt you mid-sentence to correct your pronunciation of a word. There may be no malice, but the sting of the interruption isn't small. Depending on the tone and context, this might help you refine your expression, or it might cause you to shut down.

Neutral Feedback
Someone might say, "You have such a unique way of looking at things." Is it a compliment, a dismissal, an observation? Repeated neutrality can be diplomatically useful, but it can also blur the mirror, leaving you unsure if you were seen clearly.

Ambiguous Feedback
You offer something vulnerable, and no one responds or they do so without clarity. The silence might feel deafening. Without context, ambiguous feedback can feel like being invisible, tempting us to fill the void with our own insecurities.

Each of these moments leaves a trace. With awareness, we can begin to ask: *Is this reflection accurate or inherited? Is it useful or limiting? Does it reveal me or conceal me?*

Facet 3: Inward Expression (Inner Dialogue)
The *Inward* facet is where we echo—constantly, and often unconsciously. This is the most persistent *Feedback Loop* we live inside, and because it often goes unchallenged, it shapes the story we live by.

Inward Value-Based Feedback (Judgment vs. Affirmation)
This influential form of self-talk evaluates how you experience yourself from your value and belief systems. When habitual, it defines your identity. You forget an appointment and the voice says: "You're so stupid." This is value-based feedback, assigning a permanent meaning to the self instead of addressing the event. Now contrast it with this: "I forgot to write that down. Next time, I'll set a reminder." This is a correction with awareness. It names the action, not the person. Value-based feedback isn't inherently harmful; what matters is what it reinforces and why. Or this: You show up on time for something important. You prepare. You follow

through. And you say to yourself: *"I'm proud of how I showed up today."* Still value-based, yes—but now it's specific. It affirms a behavior you chose, not a fixed identity. And that affirmation isn't about performance. It's about alignment. You're not reinforcing a persona of being a genius or the best—you're recognizing a moment of coherence with your intention and values.

Inward Corrective Feedback (From Mistake to Realignment)
This feedback addresses an action, not the self. It names a mismatch between intent and outcome. You say something that doesn't land as you hoped, and the voice notes: "That's not what you meant." This is helpful. But sometimes the correction sharpens: "You *always* do this." Now the feedback isn't about what happened; it's about who you are. The danger is its subtle potential to shift from guidance into guilt. Correction supports self-development only when paired with compassion and clarity.

Inward Neutral Feedback (Observation Without Evaluation)
This can be the most overlooked form of inner feedback. It simply notices without emotional charge. "I made the call." "I walked away." "I'm here now." These statements affirm presence and name reality without coloring it. This can be incredibly grounding. However, neutrality can drift into detached avoidance if used to flatten experience. The phrase "Whatever. It's done" is technically neutral, but the tone tells a story of resignation. When used with awareness, neutral feedback is a mirror without distortion.

Inward Ambiguous Feedback (Unclear, Contradictory, or Vague)
This is the slipperiest form of internal feedback. It sounds like something, but you're not quite sure what. "That was... fine, I guess." "Ugh, classic me." These are emotional smokescreens. They imply dissatisfaction but offer no real insight. Because they are vague, they are hard to challenge. Awareness invites a different approach: "I felt unsure in that moment, and I want to understand why." This doesn't push for an immediate answer; it opens a space for genuine insight to arise.

Facet 4: Authentic Self

The Feedback that arises from *Authentic Self* feels different. It rarely arrives with fireworks or drama. It often comes as a recognition, a clear tone that resonates and harmonizes what feels dissonant.

Authentic Feedback: When Awareness Speaks

This feedback is not *positive* or *negative* in the traditional sense; it is truthful, clear, compassionate, and coherent. Unlike the other voices that echo emotions such as pride or shame, this one doesn't ask for applause. It invites alignment. You might hear:

> "That wasn't aligned. You knew it, and you can choose again."
> "This doesn't need to be fixed, just felt and met with honesty."
> "You are not late. You are right on time for your own awareness."

This feedback doesn't reinforce identity; it reminds you of presence. It doesn't moralize; it clarifies intention. It doesn't justify; it reconnects you to your inner compass. It is the source, not an echo. When you hear it, ask yourself: Am I shrinking or seeing clearly? Is this a correction of ego or a return to essence? Sometimes, the most powerful feedback is not advice, but a stillness that says: *"You already know."*

Summary & Practice

The Architecture of Inner Feedback

Feedback is not just something we receive; it is something we constantly give ourselves. Like all architecture, it shapes the environment we live in. Some internal messages are supportive, while others are judgmental or vague. They affect your self-perception, emotional tone, and inner alignment. When you pay attention not just to what you say to yourself, but how, why, and through which facet it's expressing, you can shift from passive recipient to conscious and intentional designer. You can reconfigure the very space where experience is made, tuning your Faculties (Mastery, Awareness, Worthiness, Will, Wisdom, Oneness, and Creativity) in the process.

Feedback Loop Practice

Before sleep or first thing in the morning, try this 5-minute practice.

1. **Recall a moment** from the day when you talked to yourself about something you did, felt, or experienced.
2. **Replay your internal dialogue.** Ask: "Was the feedback I gave myself value-based, corrective, neutral, or ambiguous?" "Was it specific or generalized?" "Which facet did it reinforce?" "What did it reinforce: shame, pride, clarity, fear, compassion?"
3. **Rephrase it intentionally.** If it was harsh, make it kind and supportive. If it was vague, make it specific.
4. **Pause and Breathe.** Notice how the rephrased feedback feels. Let your body, heart, and mind register the difference.

Every feedback moment is both an ending and a beginning. Through the *Four Facets*, awareness learns to listen—to what is expressed, mirrored, echoed, and known. Each reflection returns energy to the center of being, inviting a new differentiation of experience. *Feedback* becomes the motion through which awareness refines itself, shaping how you live and create.

With this, the *Foundations* now stand as living structures. They are no longer concepts to understand but movements to inhabit—each one participating in the same rhythm of reflection and renewal. From here, we turn toward integration: the transition from knowing the Foundations to living their Flow.

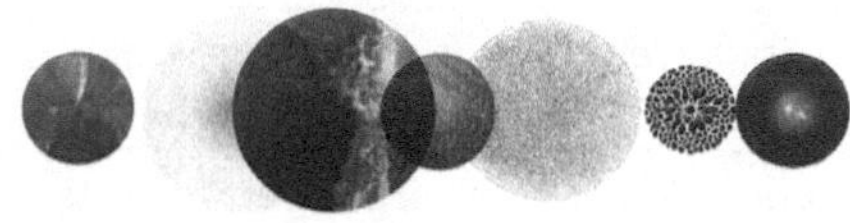

CHAPTER TEN

From Foundations to Flow

Awareness expands in layers, not ladders. There is no final version of yourself, nor a perfect order through which you must progress. The concepts you've encountered across this part of the book—verbal architecture, essence, polarity, perception, belief, experience, and the multifaceted self—are foundations to live from.

These seven models are offered as functional landmarks —perspectives that help illuminate how awareness can deepen. You may find more frameworks along your own path. Others may emerge as subsets of these. The number is not sacred. As we complete this Part and prepare to enter the next, it is useful to pause and integrate. How do these foundations help you live from a more expanded awareness? The answer is found by understanding how they support the ongoing inner process of *Self-Discovery*, *Self-Development*, *Self-Mastery*, and *Self-Knowledge*.

This integration matters because we experience ourselves across countless situations. Sometimes we're asking, "*Who am I?*" Other times, "*What do I do with this?*" The 4-S Process gives you language for these moments, and these seven *Foundations* provide context for your inquiry. Let's briefly revisit these foundations:

Model	What It Offers
Words Do Matter	Language contributes to how we structure reality. What you ask determines what you notice; what you say reinforces what you experience.
I Am	Beneath all roles is your stable and unchanging presence.
Duality and Polarity	Experience isn't binary; every state lives on a spectrum.
Perception, Viewpoint, & Perspective	You don't always see things objectively or in their entirety. Noticing your lens invites new insight.
Belief, Faith, Conviction, & Knowledge	Your inner posture shapes experience and directs where you place your attention.
Channels of Experience	Body, Mind, Heart, and Spirit—four pathways through which you engage and shape life.
Faceted BEing	Your sense of self isn't a single fixed identity but a set of facets that shift with context.

We can now see how they directly support each phase of the 4-S process:

4-S Expression	Primary Supporting Foundations	Key Contribution
Self-Discovery	Words Do Matter, Channels of Experience, Duality and Polarity	Naming what is present, noticing contrast, and sensing what is felt.
Self-Development	Belief, Faith, Conviction, and Knowledge, Perception, Viewpoint, and Perspective, Faceted BEing	Refining how you interpret, choose, and respond to what arises.
Self-Mastery	I Am, Duality and Polarity, and especially Spirit's attention + intention channel.	Acting with alignment, seeing the full spectrum, and remaining centered.
Self-Knowledge	I Am, Faceted BEing, Perception, Viewpoint, and Perspective	Seeing clearly who and what is operating within you, beneath conditioning.

> ***Note:*** *While shown here in primary alignments, every foundational model informs every phase. The connections are fluid, not fixed.*

Understanding this structure is crucial as we enter the next part of the book, which explores **Seven Faculties of Human Potential**—built-in capacities you don't acquire but simply tune and refine: *Mastery*, *Awareness*, *Worthiness*, *Will*, *Wisdom*, *Oneness*, and *Creativity*.

The *Foundations* are the scaffolding, the *4-S Process* is your evolving movement through them, and your *Faculties* are your native dynamic forces of engagement. Without awareness of the Foundations, Faculties become ideals to chase. With it, they engage with clarity. In the next part, we turn our attention to these inner instruments—the *Seven Faculties* that refine awareness into creative participation.

PART III

Seven Faculties of Human Potential

Before we explore each faculty individually, it's important to recognize how they function together as a unified, living system, heard through our *Four Channels*—Body, Mind, Heart, and Spirit (attention + intention). The shift isn't about becoming someone new, but tuning the inner instruments already within you so your outer expression is in coherence with full potential.

> ***Reminder: The Faculties do not arise from a higher version of you, nor from a separate plane of being. They are expressive capacities through which awareness engages experience, regardless of where that experience is configured.***

This is not a rigid system, nor is the number seven universal—it's a map chosen for completeness and clarity. Together they form a coherent field.

- **Mastery:** Your ability to self-govern.
- **Awareness:** Your capacity for presence, clarity, and perception.
- **Worthiness:** Your sense of value, self-regard, and inner trust.
- **Will:** Your power to direct energy and initiate movement.
- **Wisdom:** Your ability to discern, act with integrity, and flow *for* life.

- **Oneness:** Your awareness of wholeness, balance, and alignment.
- **Creativity:** Your capacity to shape, direct, and manifest experience.

As dynamic forces of engagement, *Faculties* shape how you meet life, interpret experience, and move from *intention* into lived form. But each faculty isn't a binary switch. Imagine them as ever-playing instruments, tuned rather than acquired. One moment you might play a clear note of autonomy; the next, a hesitant chord. These aren't failures but invitations to tune—the frequency and phase of how a faculty is engaged.

They play together like a musical ensemble, with *Spirit (attention + intention)* as the conductor's baton, entraining the ensemble—synchronizing each instrument into harmonic alignment. Engage *Mastery*, and it resonates through your *Will*, *Awareness*, *Worthiness*, and *Wisdom*. **The quality of your life's music depends on that real-time harmony.** In the chapters ahead, we'll explore each faculty's range, dimensions, and tuning practices.

We've embarked on a journey of expanded awareness—of *seeing*. Now we move from seeing to *tuning*—**Your orchestra is already playing. Let's tune it.**

CHAPTER ELEVEN

Mastery

The faculty of *Mastery* is not something you earn through status or struggle; it is already active within you, shaping how you lead your life, respond to challenge, and stand your ground energetically. Full *Mastery* is the state of alignment—the ability to engage your capacities with direction and steadiness. It expresses itself in how you move through feedback, friction, and change. *Mastery* is the integrative art of learning, refining, and self-governance. It's *how* you hone, calibrate, and sustain your engagement over time. In essence, *Mastery* answers the questions: "How well do I govern my movement?" "What am I learning?" "How skillfully do I execute?" "Am I free to follow my own direction?" It turns raw momentum into artful, sustainable craft.

When this faculty is tuned, you experience clarity in your decisions and integrity in how you show up. When untuned, you may fall into performance-driven behavior, over-control, or the reactive suppression of uncertainty. *Mastery* isn't about control; it's about congruence. It reveals whether your actions arise from pressure or presence. This faculty tunes *Authority*, *Teaching & Learning*, *Expertise*, and *Autonomy* into coherent expression.

Authority: Self-Governance

Authority begins with the inner posture of self-leadership, not titles or labels. It is a vibrational tone that shapes how you hold your own space, respond to feedback, and direct your choices. This expression of *Mastery* is a tone beneath every boundary you assert and every initiative you take. When *Mastery* vibrates with the tone of *Authority*, you establish the inner ground rules you live by, and you don't need permission to choose them.

This expression exists on a spectrum. When *under-expressed*, you might hesitate, defer, or self-censor. When *over-expressed*, you might force outcomes or bulldoze your way forward—driven by conformity to borrowed convictions rather than aligned intent. Both poles undermine your Authentic Self's free expression from raw potential. When *aligned*, you speak and act from a grounded presence, trusting your own voice and timing. When out of tune, your choices may feel fragmented (second-guessing), your sense of permission may hinge on others' reactions (externally dependent), and you may clutch control rigidly to mask uncertainty. *Authority* gets tuned not by tightening control, but by refining your inner signal.

Through the *4-S Process*: Notice when you yield authority out of habit (**Self-Discovery**), strengthen clarity around your values and agency (**Self-Development**), hold your field without collapsing (**Self-Mastery**), and sustain balanced *Authority* in service of your highest intent (**Self-Knowledge**).

Practice: Tuning Your Authority

Notice in Spirit (attention + intention) how you...

- **Pause before assertion:** When the urge to prove or withdraw arises, pause. Ask, "Am I speaking from presence or protection?"
- **Anchor in your why:** Let clarity of intent shape your tone—authority without clear intent is just noise.
- **Distinguish control from coherence.** True authority doesn't require force; it emerges when your words, posture, and values align.

- **Embody authority.** Notice which facet—*Outward, Mirror, Inward*, or *Authentic*—is leading as you assert yourself.

Teaching and Learning: The Calibration of Experience

This expression of *Mastery* is your intrinsic ability to integrate feedback, refine experience, and transform moments into deeper self-awareness. You're always teaching yourself something, and you're always learning something from your experiences. *Teaching and Learning* turns every outcome into feedback. This matters because the gap between your intention and the outcome of your actions always reveals something, allowing you to recalibrate.

When this expression is out of tune, you may lecture yourself without integrating, learn without applying, or project unsolicited lessons onto others. When tuned, you use humility to learn from your own life and the discipline to teach yourself from every *Feedback Loop*. You ground the idea that *Teaching* equals *Learning*, and *Learning* equals *Teaching*.

Through the *4-S Process*, you: notice the patterns between what you teach & learn and what you experience **(Self-Discovery)**, practice humility to align with your true intent **(Self-Development)**, learn from misalignment **(Self-Mastery)**, and recognize yourself as both student and teacher **(Self-Knowledge)**. The deeper insight is that *Teaching and Learning* is a calibration tool for your internal *Feedback Loop*. *Awareness* is what turns unconscious patterns into conscious tuning.

Practice: Tuning Your Teaching and Learning

Notice in Spirit (attention + intention) how you...

- **Trace the Feedback Loop:** Recognize the lesson in every loop: "What is this teaching me?"
- **Pause to fine tune:** Check in by asking yourself: "Am I willing to learn from this experience?" "Am I directing attention to learn or to defend?"
- **Reflect on Patterns:** Ask, "What themes are recurring in what I teach myself? Are they inherited scripts?"

- **Journal or Reflect:** When something doesn't land as expected, ask, "What is this moment inviting me to see differently?"

Expertise: The Precision of Practice

This expression of *Mastery* is a frequency of lived integration, emerging from how consistently you apply what you've come to understand. Think of it as the continuum from novice to expert; the novice overthinks, while the expert moves from embodied experience. This form of *Mastery* makes your inner alignment visible. *Expertise* is the natural result of tuned Self-Discipline applied over time.

When *Expertise* is out of tune, you may slip into a performance loop, pretending or lecturing without experience, or obsessing over details to the point of paralysis. In tune, it holds the principle of a Master Director: resonance without effort. The deeper insight is that *Expertise* is not just information; it's an embodiment where attention and effort stabilize into a precise waveform of skilled action. It meets each recalibration with presence and adaptability. Feedback becomes a partner and a collaborator.

This expression is honed through the *4-S Process* as you notice which steps in your practice you skip or overthink (**Self-Discovery**), set a clear intention for each practice session (**Self-Development**), hold the full cycle of repetition and adjustment under pressure, without losing composure (**Self-Mastery**), and recognize what you've earned through lived experience (**Self-Knowledge**).

Practice: Tuning Your Expertise

Notice in Spirit (attention + intention) how you...

- **Return to Repetition:** Identify a form or practice that brings you clarity and deepen your engagement there.
- **Refine Through Feedback:** Ask yourself, "Where am I seeing repeated outcomes that need recalibration?"
- **Sharpen Through Simplicity:** Choose one area to simplify. Expertise sharpens through subtraction and practice.

Autonomy: The Power to Direct Your Own Flow

Autonomy is the expression of *Mastery* through inner-directed freedom. It is the grounded ability to stand in your own presence and direct your own flow, regardless of external noise. When autonomy is tuned, you can see the space for movement, feel that you can move, and you know how to move. It allows you to act from your *I Am*, not from the expectations of others or the programs of the past, freeing you from rigid identity structures. When untuned, you may feel constricted or imprisoned; movement feels impossible or scary, and you may mistake avoidance for flow or disengagement for neutrality.

Across the *4-S Process*: you notice the implicit boundaries and where you've been confined by "shoulds" **(Self-Discovery)**, consciously remove or re-set boundaries that align with your inner frequency **(Self-Development)**, adjust those boundaries as needed to maintain free flow **(Self-Mastery)**, and hold *Autonomy* as your default state—recognizing inner freedom and worthiness as non-negotiable **(Self-Knowledge)**. *Autonomy* is the lived resonance of energetic coherence, a frequency of freedom that does not require permission to exist.

Practice: Tuning Your Autonomy

Notice in Spirit (attention + intention) how you...

- **Audit Your "Shoulds":** Notice how often your actions begin with a "should." Pause, ask why, and shift your attention to inner permission.
- **Reclaim a Micro-Decision:** Find one small choice you've deferred and own it fully.
- **Test Non-Conformity:** Gently act outside a usual social pattern and simply observe how it feels in your heart and body.
- **Breathe Into Center:** Before making a choice, take one centering breath and ask, "Am I choosing this from inner freedom and worthiness?"

The Interconnected Flow of Mastery

These four expressions of Mastery—*Authority*, *Teaching and Learning*, *Expertise*, and *Autonomy*—are not separate skills to acquire in sequence. They are an interwoven system of coherence. *Authority* strengthens *Teaching and Learning*; *Teaching and Learning* deepens *Expertise*; *Expertise* reinforces *Autonomy*; *Autonomy* clarifies and grounds *Authority*. This creates a spiraling dynamic of *Mastery*—entrained by *Spirit*'s guiding focus—rather than a static, stage-based structure. They are constantly informing and supporting one another. Tuning your faculty of Mastery is to consciously engage this entire system, helping you channel universal potential into a focused form.

This dynamic faculty of Mastery strengthens your ability to self-govern. But to govern your inner world, seeing it clearly is key. This leads us to our next exploration: the faculty of *Awareness*.

CHAPTER TWELVE

AWARENESS

The faculty of *Awareness* is not something you acquire; it's the ever-present capacity you recognize and choose to live from. It's your built-in ability to notice, to be fully present, and to perceive directly. Unlike intellect or intuition—which interpret and analyze—*Awareness* simply witnesses. It is the light by which all other inner movements become visible.

Without tuned *Awareness*, your attention is hijacked by habit, identity, emotion, or limiting beliefs. With *Awareness*, you gain the pause that makes choice possible. Until you become conscious of a pattern, you cannot redirect it. Attuning to awareness isn't about fixing a flaw, but about coming into phase with what is happening *now*. It expands your range of perception (frequency), brings your inner timing into sync with reality (phase alignment), and binds Body, Mind, Heart, and Spirit into one coherent perceiver (coupling strength). When your system feels fragmented—thoughts outrunning feelings, attention balking at action—*Awareness* reunites all channels into a single field of presence.

Consciousness: The Expression of Presence Realization

This expression of Awareness is the lived sense of "I Am that I Am"—the anchor of Awareness itself. It is more than clear seeing; it is remembering who is doing the seeing. It is the ground-state witness that underlies every perception; the movement to recognize yourself as the ever-present observer before any story begins. Consciousness stabilizes you in presence so that distortion cannot hijack your experience. It distinguishes raw data from interpretation—holding space before meaning arises.

When in tune, you discern what belongs to you and what is simply passing through. You feel grounded in presence even as thoughts, feelings, and roles shift around you. In Chapter 15, we will review the Faculty of *Wisdom's* expression that supports this realization. When out of tune, you live inside a narrow or distorted reality: mind locked in judgments or imposed narratives, emotions overwhelm observation, identities tell you who you are, or your body feels present while your mind drifts onto familiar, yet isolating and minimizing ideas.

Through the *4-S Process*, you: notice when you're nonconscious of the watcher—the "I" who notices **(Self-Discovery)**, practice pausing at the edge of reaction to claim presence before narrating **(Self-Development)**, sustain the witness even amidst strong sensations or complex situations **(Self-Mastery)**, and recognize how remembering *I Am* has reshaped your experience over time **(Self-Knowledge)**.

Practice: Tuning Your Clarity

Notice in Spirit (attention + intention) how you...

- **Pause Before Interpretation:** The instant you sense a strong reaction, stop. Ask, "Who is the silent 'I' noticing right now?"
- **Recalibrate to the Senses:** Anchor in one unreported detail—three ambient sounds, a breeze on your skin, or the play of light on a surface.

- **Open Inquiry:** Pose non-leading questions: "What might be here that I'm not seeing?" or "Where is my focus, and why?"
- **Lens Adjustment:** Zoom in on a single element ("What precisely is happening?") then zoom out ("What larger context does this fit into?").
- **Return with Breath:** One fully conscious inhale and exhale can reinstate the sense of *I Am* more effectively than any analysis.

With *Consciousness* tuned, you reclaim the foundational *I Am* as your constant ground—so every subsequent faculty can play its part in coherent harmony.

Mindfulness: The Expression of Embodied Presence

This expression of *Awareness* isn't about mastering a technique; it's about recognizing the capacity to deliberately place your attention in the present moment, to *what is*. *Mindfulness* is the expression that allows you to return, again and again, to embodied presence. It shows up in how you breathe, hold your posture, and how fully you inhabit what is here.

When this expression is in tune, you focus attention on what's happening right now, you acknowledging what is present with acceptance, and you are aware that you're being aware—recognizing when your mind has wandered and gently returning attention to the present when needed. When out of tune, your attention gets pulled out into cycles of distraction, detachment, or dissociation, perhaps getting caught up in past regrets or future anxieties. You tend to categorize experiences as good or bad, right or wrong. These are not flaws; they are invitations—feedback signals showing you where presence dwells.

Through the *4-S Process*, you: notice the moments when you feel present—or absent **(Self-Discovery)**, practice returning to the now through breath, posture, and awareness of sensation **(Self-Development)**, observe your shifts and return to present-moment awareness **(Self-Mastery)**, maintain acceptance and shift to the present without judgment **(Self-Knowledge)**.

Practice: Tuning Your Mindfulness
Notice in Spirit (attention + intention) how you...

- **Breath Awareness:** Focus attention on your natural breathing pattern without trying to change it. Breath is always available and happening in the present moment.
- **Body Scan Meditation:** Systematically direct attention through different parts of your body, from toes to head.
- **Name the Moment:** Use verbal cues to tune attention into embodiment: "I am here." "This is my breath." "These are the sensations I'm noticing."
- **Micro-Presence Check:** Set a gentle cue to check in periodically: "Where is my attention?" "What is my intention?" "What am I feeling?"

Passion: The Expression of Energized Engagement

Passion, as we explore it here, is the expression of fully engaging with your experience—on purpose, with presence, toward a sense of excitement and belonging. It is the energized current of your *attention and intention* meeting the world, a willingness to participate with depth and enthusiasm. When this engagement flows from a state of inner *Alignment* (as we'll explore in the faculty of Oneness), it manifests as pure joy and fulfillment. You're already engaging in every moment, but not all of it is fully conscious, intentional, or with your full attention and willingness. *Passion* brings the spotlight of awareness into the act of living, so your participation becomes a deliberate expression of being—bringing frequency from your *Authentic Self* and phase into embodied action. It is what happens when *Awareness* becomes action—when *Spirit (attention + intention)* and *being* meet action, and Body, Mind, and Heart are engaged in harmony toward joy and fulfillment.

When *Passion* is out of tune, engagement becomes scattered, forced, or absent. You may feel burned out, disconnected, avoiding full presence, or feel you're just going through the motions. You lose curiosity and drive. This is often a sign that your engagement isn't congruent with your authentic *why*.

In the *4-S Process*, tuning Passion looks like noticing what you give your energy to (**Self-Discovery**), practicing deliberate engagement in moments that matter (**Self-Development**), aligning your presence with your priorities (**Self-Mastery**), and recognizing how your engagement patterns reflect your internal landscape (**Self-Knowledge**).

Practice: Tuning Your Engagement
Notice in Spirit (attention + intention) how you...

- **Re-center Before Action:** Pause before entering a task or interaction. Ask, "Am I truly here for this?" Then, bring your full attention into the moment, recognizing how it affects you emotionally.
- **Anchor with Intention:** Attach a one-word intention to what you're about to do (e.g. focus, care, exciting). Let this guide how you engage.
- **Reclaim from Auto-Pilot:** Notice when you're acting out of compulsion or habit. Pause, name what's driving you, and consciously choose whether to continue.
- **Track Energy Matching:** After a significant interaction, ask, "Did my action match my actual intent?" "Did it reinforce joy, excitement, and fulfillment?" If not, adjust for next time.

Insight: The Expression of Inner Illumination

This expression is your inherent capacity to illuminate patterns, motivations, and meaning already present in your lived experience. *Insight* is active every time you pause, reflect, and notice what was hidden. It is not the same as intellect or analysis; it is a tuning mechanism that reveals coherence by shedding light on the deeper currents shaping a moment. Without *Insight*, experiences accumulate but don't integrate.

When *Insight* is out of tune, clarity dims. Instead of inner illumination, you may find yourself caught in loops of confusion, overthinking, or misreading situations by attributing distorted or subconscious intent. These are signals inviting you to gently retune.

You don't force insight; you create the conditions for it to emerge. This means allowing space between perception and interpretation, returning to see the patterns behind repeated experiences, and letting reflection be embodied. When in tune, *Insight* allows you to perceive and realign with your *Authentic Self*—cutting through noise and distortion. Insight refines coupling strength by illuminating hidden motives or missed lessons.

Through the *4-S Process*, you: pause and recognize previously unseen patterns and internal narratives (**Self-Discovery**), cultivate the ability to pause, reflect, and inquire without distortion (**Self-Development**), bring light into every moment and recalibrate action and response in real time (**Self-Mastery**), and fuse insight with your *I Am's* unconditional nature (**Self-Knowledge**).

Practice: Tuning Your Insight

Notice in Spirit (attention + intention) how you...

- **Pause with what feels incomplete:** Ask, "Is there more to this than I've seen so far?"
- **Use questions that open, not close:** Replace "What's wrong with me?" with "What is this showing me?"
- **Try an Evening Flashback:** Before sleep, revisit your day not to judge it, but to trace where awareness opened. Where did something become clearer?
- **Practice Intentioned Revisit.** Pick one unresolved moment and return to it with the sole intent of learning, not fixing. See what's present now that wasn't then.

The Interconnected Flow of Awareness

The four expressions of Awareness—*Consciousness*, *Mindfulness*, *Passion*, and *Insight*—form a recursive, mutually reinforcing spiral. Each expression both arises from and deepens the others: *Consciousness* anchors you in the ever-present *I Am*, creating the stable ground for direct noticing. *Mindfulness* places that anchored awareness into your lived experience. *Passion* brings energy of excitement and aliveness to what you do. *Insight* arises from that wholehearted engagement, revealing new depths of

I Am and fresh patterns to observe. In turn, each *Insight* deepens your understanding of presence, which further refines your *Consciousness*—and the cycle begins again at a more subtle level. This is *Awareness* in motion: a continuous spiral of grounding, embodiment, engagement, and illumination.

This faculty of Awareness—in all its expressions—is the light by which we see our inner world. But this clarity and presence naturally illuminate another core faculty: our intrinsic sense of value. To *see* clearly is one thing; to *feel that you are worthy of what you see* is another. We now turn to the faculty of *Worthiness*.

CHAPTER THIRTEEN

WORTHINESS

There is no condition, performance, or external approval required for *worthiness*. It is not earned, given, or measured—it is remembered, recognized, and expressed. In this model, we distinguish between two essential aspects: *Intrinsic Worthiness*—the simple fact that existence itself affirms your value, entirely independent of merit—and *Worthiness* as a *Faculty*, which is your capacity to attune to that truth and express it through how you live.

This faculty is a dynamic mechanism that tunes how fully your experience resonates with your inherent value. Through it, you sense where you've withheld love from yourself or internalized others' judgments over your own knowing. When tuned, there is no confusion between external achievement and internal value, between merit and worth. When untuned, you may feel the need to prove, apologize for, or withhold your self—imagining you're not deserving, worthy, or enough. Tuning this faculty restores perception to the raw potential from which your worth emerges. **You no longer act to become someone of value; you act because you already are.**

Self-Esteem: The Expression of Internal Foundation

Self-esteem is not about superiority or certainty. It's the lived sense that you *are*—and therefore are worthy—before doing, proving, or comparing. And because you recognized it, especially in contrast to what denies it, it becomes like your own inner achievement. This doesn't mean entitlement; it means coherence.

When *Self-Esteem* is in tune, your actions are no longer trying to justify your value or worth, but begin to reflect them. Your sense of self-worth inspires you to add value to what you create, what you choose, and what you manifest, because they honor your inherent potential. When this expression is out of tune, you may constantly measure your worth and the value of your expressions against others' approval, feeling the need to prove, compete, or shrink from opportunities. This often shows up as one of two distortions: *self-inflation* to override insecurity or reaffirm an identity, or *self-erasure* to avoid being seen as someone you believe is less. Both are compensatory.

The *4-S Process* helps ground this expression as you: notice how your worth has been externally shaped and the criteria used to measure value (**Self-Discovery**), reframe your self-perception around your intrinsic worth (**Self-Development**), embody confidence without needing comparison (**Self-Mastery**), and recognize your worth and value as independent of any role (**Self-Knowledge**).

Practice: Tuning Your Self-Esteem

Self-esteem is tuned by removing the internal conditions you've placed on it. Notice in Spirit (attention + intention) how you...

- **Track Your Default** Why: Ask, "Why am I doing, thinking, or feeling this? Is it to prove worth, seek approval, avoid judgment—or is it simply aligned with who I am?"
- **Speak Without a Sales Pitch:** Practice expressing preferences or boundaries with simple clarity, without over-explaining. Watch for the reflex to convince.
- **Mirror Work, Reimagined:** Stand before a mirror and say with presence: "I am. I am enough. I am worthy. I deserve."

Breathe. Let it land. Then say, "I choose how I live this enoughness."

Self-Love: The Expression of Radiant Embrace

This expression reflects a deep resonance of appreciation and affection for your whole being. *Self-love* isn't a reward; it's the natural bloom of recognition: *I am worthy of love, including my own.* When tuned, it means you include *yourself* in your circle of compassion, protection, treasure, and care—not as an afterthought or something earned, and with no need to ask for permission or apologize. Your inner dialogue shifts, care becomes natural, and the space to heal opens.

The mere realization of your existence fuels the highest and most consistent expressions of every faculty. This internal state of *Self-Love* is the foundation. Later, in the faculty of *Wisdom*, we will explore how this expands into Love as an active, unifying force in the world.

When untuned, *Self-Love* hides in subtleties: you may love others easily but doubt you are lovable without proof; you forgive others but replay your own regrets; you expect excellence from yourself while making room for others' shortcomings. You may interpret "taking care of yourself" as selfishness, entitlement, or egoism, and feel guilty when tending to yourself. Similarly, you may project your own sense of lack onto others and feel the need to add value to your existence through performance, leading to the obsession to compare with and compete for what you believe is missing.

Through the *4-S Process*, you: realize how you've placed yourself outside your own circle of care or if your focus and intent is directed toward persona or identity (**Self-Discovery**); practice acts of genuine self-nourishment (**Self-Development**); protect and nurture love toward yourself while honoring care and respect for others (**Self-Mastery**); and live from an inner field of unconditional acceptance (**Self-Knowledge**).

A Word on Which I'll Make an Exception
I've avoided drawing from religion in this book, but for Self-Love, I will make one exception. You've likely heard the phrase: "Love your neighbor as yourself." Many interpret this as an instruction to treat others the way you'd like to be treated. But look again at the original phrase. It doesn't say *instead of* yourself, *more than* yourself, or to show how *loving* you are. It says *as* yourself. Which means: *love yourself too*. That's the measure. That's the invitation. It implies that self-love is the very soil in which healthy engagement with the world can grow. It doesn't mean you're better or worse than others. It means you are included in the field of compassion. It means you are allowed to rest, to feel, to forgive, to be forgiven, to care for yourself, and to exist as you are.

Practice: Tuning Your Self-Love
Notice in Spirit (attention + intention) how you...

- **Mirror Presence:** Each morning, meet your reflection and say, "I love you. I care for you. I forgive you" — and mean it.
- **Reverse the Inner Talk:** Catch yourself in a moment of harsh internal dialogue. Ask, "Would I speak to a loved one this way?" Offer yourself that same tone of care.
- **Reclaim "Deserve":** When something good happens, instead of thinking *I do or don't deserve this*, try saying: "I receive this." This bypasses the logic of merit and restores worthiness without a condition to earning it.

Self-Compassion: The Expression of Tender Presence

Self-Compassion is the gentle willingness to meet your own humanity with care. It's not indulgence or excuse—it's the grace that allows healing, acceptance, and movement. When tuned, this expression allows you to soften around pain, offer understanding without judgement, and recognize the shared humanness in people—*including yourself*. It reframes deserving from judgement and condemnation to grace and opportunity. In *Worthiness*, *Self-Compassion* is how your inner value becomes visible in motion.

There was a saying I picked up somewhere many years ago: *"Mercy is not giving to someone what they deserve. Grace is giving to someone what they don't deserve."* Originally, the saying was used in the context of condemnation and salvation, or in simple terms: mercy withholds punishment when it is deserved, and grace offers salvation even when it is not deserved. Here, let's fuse both mercy and grace while removing the frame of punishment altogether. *Self-Compassion* becomes the conscious disposition to extend mercy and grace to yourself as a form of active *course correction*. Compassion becomes a key part of the *Feedback Loop*—meant not to imprison, but to set you free. It supports rehabilitation without condemnation and opens the path to realignment.

Self-Compassion also steers away from mere justification. It is not an excuse, but a way to restore inner alignment through self-responsibility and accountability. This is how empathy supports healing. The *Authentic Self* observes your experience with unconditional presence. It doesn't take sides, but with each feedback loop, when you are aligned, you're able to see what no longer serves and what continues to steer you toward collapse.

When *Self-Compassion* is out of tune, you may suppress pain, harden around mistakes, or outsource tenderness to others. You may show compassion outwardly but not inwardly. *Self-Compassion* says, "I see your struggle."

Through the *4-S Process*: notice how your intent shifts when you don't meet your own expectations (**Self-Discovery**), focus on course correction with kindness (**Self-Development**), remain soft and open even in moments of challenge (**Self-Mastery**), and recognize how compassion has become your default mode of meeting experience (**Self-Knowledge**).

Practice: Tuning Your Self-Compassion with Tender Presence
Notice in Spirit (attention + intention) how you...

- **Pause when Discomfort Arises:** Breathe before responding to yourself. Ask, "What is really being felt here?" Avoid rushing to fix or flee.

- **Offer a Simple Phrase of Inner Kindness:** When in self-judgment, pause and say, "Of course this hurts. You're allowed to feel hurt."
- **Place a Hand Over Your Heart:** Gesture reassurance with self-contact.
- **Choose Mercy and Grace:** Notice where judgment masquerades as discipline. Choose mercy. Choose grace.

Beauty & Elegance: The Expression of Confidence from Worth

This last expression is about how your intrinsic value becomes perceptible—how the unseen worth is made visible through presence, movement, and form. *Beauty*, in this context, is not about appearance; it is the felt sense of harmony that emerges when your expression aligns with your essence. The focus is on the beauty of the system more than a physical comparison of social origin. *Elegance*, as beautifully described in Paulo Coelho's *Manuscripts Found in Accra,* is not extravagance; it is simplicity paired with depth, precision without effort, the ability to carry complexity with clarity. It is an internal quality that manifests externally through action and bearing, where true elegance is found in sobriety and simplicity, in precise movement executed with grace, and in a state of being characterized by discretion, respect, and kindness. Together, they form a way of *walking through life* that reflects inner worth and value with no need to prove it. *Beauty & Elegance* are the outer expression of self-respect and inner coherence.

When this expression is out of tune, you might feel discomfort with being seen as who you don't want to be seen, or have a tendency to over-display, directly dictating the need to shape the *Outward*, *Social*, and *Inward Facets of BEing* as "someone else." You may dress, speak, or act in ways that feel performative rather than authentic. You may confuse complexity or excess for depth or meaning. You may live with a constant need to attach value to yourself with possessions, knowledge, power, or behavior. Tuning your *Beauty & Elegance* is about cultivating habits that elevate your *Authentic* expression.

Through the *4-S Process*: Notice the excess of how you express yourself and how it reflects your inner sense of worth and value (**Self-Discovery**), cultivate habits and practices that elevate your Authentic Self's expression without performance (**Self-Development**), bring elegance to your presence by living from *Authenticity* and its potential (**Self-Mastery**), recognize that confidence is internal, and worth doesn't need adornment (**Self-Knowledge**).

Practice: Tuning Your Beauty & Elegance
Notice in Spirit (attention + intention) how you...

- **Simplify to Reveal:** Sort through the superfluous. Instead of adding more, ask, "Why am I adding? What's essential?"
- **Graciously Listen and Acknowledge:** Practice shifting the focus from being *interesting* to being *interested*. This applies to others and to yourself.
- **Journaling Alignment:** Spend five minutes at the end of the day and ask, "When did I feel most like myself today? When did I feel least like myself today?"
- **Practice Poised Presence:** Perform a simple posture check throughout the day. Standing and moving with poise sends a powerful signal to your brain—and to others—that you are confident, present, and self-assured.

The Coherence of Worthiness

The faculty of *Worthiness* draws on all seven of the foundational models we explored in Part II, providing both the grounding and the tuning needed to experience unconditional value.

Foundational Model	Contribution to Worthiness
I Am	Establishes that worthiness is intrinsic and not earned.
The Faceted BEing	Reveals how worth can be distorted across the Outward, Mirror, and Inward facets.
Perception, Viewpoint, & Perspective	Helps identify and expand limiting narratives about worth, value and self-perception.

Foundational Model	Contribution to Worthiness
The Channels of Experience	Shows how worthiness is experienced through the physical, mental, emotional, and intentional channels.
Words Do Matter	Offers precision in how you speak to and about yourself, which shapes self-worth.
Belief, Faith, Conviction, & Knowledge	Tracks how belief in one's own worth and value generates the conviction to express it and the quality of what you manifest.
Duality and Polarity	Guides awareness out of dualistic self-judgment (worthy/unworthy) and into fluid alignment.

Each expression of *Worthiness* arises from and reinforces the others. *Self-Esteem* offers the foundation sense of internal value, supporting *Self-Love*. *Self-Love* nurtures *Self-Esteem* and fuels *Self-Compassion*. *Self-Compassion* applies the grace of *Self-Love*, which in turn allows for the confident expression of *Beauty & Elegance*. *Beauty & Elegance* translates the invisible into visible, allowing worth to be expressed with confidence, then circles back to *Self-Esteem*. This creates a living current of *Worthiness* that can be experienced, shared, and continually recalibrated.

To live from a place of intrinsic worthiness is to build your life on solid ground. This foundation allows for the free and conscious direction of your energy—no longer needing to prove worth and value, but to move from them. This leads us directly to the next great faculty: the power to direct that energy with focus and clarity—*Will*.

CHAPTER FOURTEEN

WILL

While *willpower* typically refers to self-control, maintaining discipline in pursuit of long-term goals, and the resistance of temptation, the faculty of *Will* is something more. It is not about forcing discipline or suppressing desire. It is the creative and dynamic force of your inner determination. This is the *power of will* itself: a deep, directive capacity that moves energy with focused intent. It does not strain; it steers. It does not overpower; it aligns.

You already have willpower—it may simply be directed toward hidden goals. You might say, "I want to stop getting angry," or "I want to change this," yet a deeper, unexamined intention—to preserve a familiar identity or soothe an old wound—continues to steer your energy. Consider why you might be directing your free will toward continuing to get angry or act that way. *Will* as such creative and dynamic force is already part of your internal system, shaping every choice and direction.

When tuned with *Awareness*, it becomes a stabilizing and initiating force you use to course-correct, commit, and engage differently. At its most refined, *Will* flows from clarity, not urgency.

It holds direction without rigidity and allows presence without passivity. When out of tune, *Will* can show up as collapse (inertia or indecision) or compulsion (over-control or burnout). When tuned, it is your instrument of intentional movement and autonomous motivation.

In this chapter, we'll explore how the faculty of *Will* steers your life through four expressions: *Self-Discipline, Intentionality, Choice,* and *Courage*. Together, they compose your capacity to direct energy with integrity.

Self-Discipline: The Expression of Sustained Focus

Self-Discipline is the force that transforms intention into consistent action. It is often mischaracterized as restriction, but in its form from expanded awareness, Self-Discipline is the chosen commitment to alignment. It is the unwavering guide that ensures your energy is directed toward what truly matters. True freedom is not the absence of discipline; it is the result of *Self-Discipline* applied with awareness.

Self-Discipline is the steady rhythm that holds your *why* in phase with your *how*. In energetic terms, it brings the frequency of repeated effort into harmony with your intention, aligns the phase of your daily choices with your larger direction, and strengthens the coupling between your focus (attention) and your drive (intention). When finely tuned, it feels like a low hum of momentum—effortless persistence rather than forced endurance; the ability to direct your energy freely, clearly, and consistently. When it's out of tune, your energy either dissipates in scattered and forced starts or locks into a rigid grind.

This expression is honed through the *4-S Process* as you: Notice your automatic patterns—where you commit to something without a coherent awareness of why (**Self-Discovery**), practice sustaining small, repeated actions with aligned intent (**Self-Development**), recalibrate when momentum falters rather than pushing harder or quitting entirely (**Self-Mastery**), and recognize when discipline becomes effortless because your commitment is to the conscious outcome (**Self-Knowledge**).

Practice: Tuning Your Self-Discipline

Notice in Spirit (attention + intention) how you...

- **Rhythmically Anchor:** Pair your discipline practice with a daily cue (same time, place, or trigger) so your system learns to enter a focused mode automatically.
- **Phase-Check Intervals:** Every hour, take 30 seconds to bring your current task into phase with your overarching intention. Ask, "Is this in phase with my larger goal?"
- **Build Frequency:** Choose a simple habit (one push-up, one page of reading) and do it three times daily. Track how the frequency of practice strengthens your capacity over a week.

Intentionality: The Expression of Aligned Action

Intentionality is the tuning force that moves *Will* from brute effort into deliberate alignment. It is the invisible architecture of purpose—the *why* that silently shapes the *how*. If *Authority* is the state of being your own leader, *Intentionality* is aligning a specific action with that leadership. Everyone holds intentions, but not all are clear; some are inherited, reactive, or masked. This expression of *Will* invites you to illuminate those currents and ask: *What is guiding this action?*

When *Intentionality* is misaligned, you may act out of pressure instead of authentic intent, say *yes* without resonance, or pursue goals that no longer feel like yours. You are moving, but the *why* is unclear or purposely hidden.

This expression manifests across the 4-S Process as you notice when your actions match your inner intention (**Self-Discovery**), practice choosing before reacting and clarifying before acting (**Self-Development**), honor the resolute "yes" or "no" that comes from congruence (**Self-Mastery**), and close the gap between surface intention and deeper alignment (**Self-Knowledge**). When this expression is attuned, even small actions feel clear. You move from a place that doesn't need to be proven.

Practice: Tuning Your Intentionality
Notice in Spirit (attention + intention) how you...

- **Pre-Action Check-In:** Before beginning a task, ask, "What do I truly intend here—and is there any quieter intention beneath my stated goal?" Pause and seek a clear alignment.
- **Reframe in One Line:** Try reducing your intention to a single phrase: "I am doing this to contribute..." or "I am doing this to express..." Simple language clarifies complex motives.
- **Remove the Residue:** When an action ends, take 10 seconds to breathe and ask: "Did that feel in coherence with your intention?" Notice without judgment.

Choice: The Expression of Empowered Selection

Choice is the moment *Will* becomes real. It is the point of action where intention takes form. Choice is the moment where the potential of *Autonomy* becomes a specific, concrete action. Every time you choose, you are shaping not just your path, but the creative capacity of who you are. We explore choice here as an expression of the faculty of *Will*—an innate power that can be tuned. You are choosing all the time; the act of deferring, avoiding, or defaulting is still a choice, just one made with attention placed elsewhere.

When this expression is out of tune, it may feel like drifting, numbing through indecision, feeling trapped, overthinking followed by regret or reactivity, or outsourcing your agency to others—even subtly. This often comes from a mismatch between attention and intention, or even attention minus intention or intention minus attention. For example, scrolling without purpose is attention minus a clear intention; making a rigid plan but never engaging with focus is intention minus attention.

This expression of *Will* is strengthened through the *4-S Process* as you notice how often you choose by default (**Self-Discovery**), practice conscious selection by ensuring you have full attention and clear intention (**Self-Development**), learn to choose with integrity under pressure (**Self-Mastery**), and see how your choices reveal deeper patterns (**Self-Knowledge**). When *Choice* is tuned, you feel awake within your own life. You choose with clarity rather than simply react, and the space between impulse and action reveals your true freedom.

Practice: Tuning Your Choice

Notice in Spirit (attention + intention) how you...

- **Reclaim Small Choices:** Before selecting what to eat, wear, or say, pause for a breath and ask: "Am I choosing this, or repeating it?"
- **Practice Micro-Agency:** In one interaction each day, consciously choose to listen with full attention and the intention of actually listening without expectation, then wait before responding.
- **Audit a Routine:** Pick one regular pattern (your morning scroll, your default response to a certain person). Ask,"Is this chosen, or assumed?" "Is this strategy, tactic, or a choice from presence?"
- **Track Inner Impact:** After making a deliberate choice, take 30 seconds to feel its imprint in your body. Do you feel more anchored or more dissonant?

Courage: The Expression of Forward Momentum

As mentioned in previous chapters, *Courage* is often reduced to the absence of fear. I propose it is not. Here, fear focuses on what might go wrong, and courage focuses on what might emerge. It is the capacity to move toward the unknown with trust in new possibilities. In this model, *Courage* is the directional force of *Will* in motion. It is the act of forward engagement despite not having full clarity of outcome or control. It is the moment you decide to lean in, even if part of you wants to retreat. Consider *Courage* as a conduit toward possibility.

When the *Courage* expression is untuned, you may find yourself over-preparing but never acting, waiting for fear to disappear before taking a step, or seeing only risks, not rewards. *Choice* becomes a burden. You let the unknown shrink your view of what's possible. When tuned, *Courage* couples with *Faith Force* to focus on possibility. Of course, it is not about irresponsibility or not diagnosing risks; *Courage* here is about the *Flow of Existence* and ensuring all possibilities are considered when choosing towards your desired outcome.

This is refined through the 4-S Process as you: realize how fear narrows your options (**Self-Discovery**), shift from fear-based prediction to possibility-based curiosity (**Self-Development**), act without waiting for absolute certainty (**Self-Mastery**), and recognize courage as your natural momentum, grounded by expertise (**Self-Knowledge**). Courage doesn't mean you stop feeling fear; it means your focus is no longer ruled by it.

Practice: Tuning Your Courage

Notice in Spirit (attention + intention) how you...

- **Shift the Frame:** When you notice a thought like, "What if this goes wrong?" reframe it with, "What if something useful or unexpected comes from this?"
- **Reframe the Action:** Instead of "What if I fail?", try: "What might I learn by doing this?" This turns a test into an exploration and brings courage to the *now*.
- **Change the Language (Verbal Architecture):** Notice how your language shapes your experience. Instead of "I can't see the path," try "Each step will help me see more."
- **Use Micro-Bravery:** Each day, act on one small decision that includes uncertainty. Make the call. Say the truth. Try the unfamiliar.

The Interconnected Flow of Will

These four expressions of Will—*Self-Discipline*, *Intentionality*, *Choice*, and *Courage*—operate not as separate skills but as a spiraling, mutually reinforcing cycle. *Self-Discipline* builds the muscle to set clear *intentions*. A clear *intention* makes it easier to *choose* wisely. A decisive *choice* generates the *courage* to follow through. And *courageous* follow-through deepens your trust in the process, which in turn reinforces your capacity for *discipline*. This creates a feedback loop where each expression tunes and energizes the next, resulting in a living, dynamic faculty of *Will*.

The faculty of *Will* gives us the power to direct our energy with clarity and integrity. It is the engine of conscious change. But direction without discernment can be misguided. To steer our lives effectively, *Will* benefits from being informed by a deeper understanding of life's patterns, rhythms, and insights. This is where our journey turns next: to the faculty of *Wisdom*.

CHAPTER FIFTEEN

Wisdom

Wisdom is not reserved for the few. It is an innate capacity already at play within you—one that can be tuned, clarified, and expressed through the choices you make every day. It is both the stillness beneath the noise and the capacity to respond from that stillness when life becomes loud.

I learned this firsthand during my military service. It was nightfall, and I had guard duty on the highest peak of a remote mountain range. The skies were clear, moonless, and the stars felt impossibly close. Then, a cloud came. Not above us, but through us. In seconds, visibility turned into imperceptible contrast. I stretched out my arm and couldn't even see my own hand. The cloud didn't obscure the racing thoughts, the spike of anxiety. "If I can't see my hand, will I see the enemy?" Then again, if I couldn't see, neither could they. The enemy never came that night. The cloud passed. Clarity returned.

Wisdom isn't just about seeing outward clearly; it's about learning to walk confidently when vision fails. *It is the clarity of knowing the cloud will pass.* In this chapter, we explore how the faculty of *Wisdom* guides your life through five expressions: *Truth*, *Virtue*, *Reciprocity*, *Dance/Flow*, and *Love*.

Truth: The Expression of Discerning Awareness

This expression of *Wisdom* is not about having the right answer. It is the capacity to refine perception by noticing what clouds it. *Truth*, as a faculty, sharpens awareness by clearing away distortion—assumptions, inherited beliefs, emotional overlays, or social conditioning—that interfere with what is actually present. It functions less as a destination and more as a tuning mechanism. Its purpose is not to arrive at certainty, but to clear the lens so your deeper knowing can guide you.

Truth filters without judgment. It recognizes the noise without being overtaken by it. When this expression is tuned, you are sensitive to subtle cues and can perceive what resonates from within rather than react to what appears on the surface. When out of tune, you may confuse clarity with control, mistake emotional intensity for accuracy, or cling to rigid conclusions in place of lived discernment.

Through the *4-S Process*, you: observe how you form conclusions (**Self-Discovery**), refine your lens by questioning what clouds perception (**Self-Development**), discern without collapsing into judgment or self-protection (**Self-Mastery**), and know when you are aligned and when you are not—without force or justification (**Self-Knowledge**).

Practice: Tuning Your Discernment

Notice in Spirit (attention + intention) how you...

- **Calibrate to the Present:** Rather than asking, "What's the absolute truth?", begin with "What is here now?" and "What am I filtering this through?"
- **Pause Before Defining:** When discomfort arises, resist quick conclusions. Ask, "What else might be true here?"
- **Notice Language of Finality:** Soften rigid self-talk. Shift from "That's just how I am" to "That's how I've been seeing it."

- **Distinguish Signal vs. Echo:** Ask, "Is this an immediate perception or a replay of a familiar narrative echoing through memory?"

Virtue: The Expression of Aligned Integrity

Virtue, in this context, is not a set of imposed moral codes, but the felt coherence between your values, your awareness, and your actions. It is a tuning force for integrity. To tune this expression of Wisdom is to bring those three into consonance. There is less tension between what you say, what you do, and what you believe. When this expression is out of tune, the dissonance often registers as internal conflict; you say yes when you mean no, or defend what you don't truly believe. Aligned integrity is not static perfection; it is dynamic congruence, tuned moment by moment. *Dynamic congruence* means your alignment shifts fluidly as your awareness deepens.

In the *4-S Process*, you: notice where your actions align—or don't—with your deeper values (**Self-Discovery**), practice consistency between word, thought, and deed (**Self-Development**), remain adaptable and principled under pressure (**Self-Mastery**), and know what integrity feels like in your system (**Self-Knowledge**).

Practice: Tuning Your Aligned Integrity

Notice in Spirit (attention + intention) how you...

- **Pause for Integrity:** Before deciding, ask, "What matters most to me here? Does this action align with my values?"
- **Inquire with Reflection:** At the end of a day, consider a moment you acted out of alignment. Kindly explore: "Was I trying to avoid conflict? What deeper belief wanted to be lived?" The goal isn't shame; it's discernment.
- **Shift Verbal Architecture:** Pay attention to how your words reflect your values. Shift from "I have to..." to "I choose to..." This moves your speech from resignation to responsibility and from scripts to sovereignty.
- **Practice what Feels True:** In a conversation, notice a moment you feel tempted to hide your values. What would it feel like to express them with clarity and care?

Reciprocity: The Expression of Relational Understanding

Reciprocity is not a transaction; it is a rhythm—a flow of energy that honors both giving and receiving as essential aspects of wisdom. This expression tunes your awareness to that flow. *Reciprocity* echoes the natural world, where life moves in tides. *Giving* and *receiving* are not opposites; they are expressions of the same current moving in and out, like breath. To block either pole is to create internal discord. To open both channels is to allow the current of life and love to circulate unhindered.

When this expression is out of tune, the flow becomes distorted through over-giving, guardedness, or hidden expectations. *Giving* may come from a need to prove your value, while *receiving* may be blocked by pride or a feeling of unworthiness. When *Reciprocity* is tuned, *giving* flows from overflow rather than depletion, and you *receive* with grace, acknowledging the gifts life offers.

In the *4-S Process*, you: recognize that both giving and receiving are natural movements of being (**Self Discovery**), practice choosing balance over compulsion (**Self-Development**), attune to the natural rhythm of *giving and receiving*, sensing when to open, when to yield, and when to hold (**Self-Mastery**), and sense the integrity of mutual nourishment as a dynamic exchange that honors the lived connection between beings (**Self-Knowledge**).

Practice: Tuning Your Reciprocity

Notice in Spirit (attention + intention) how you...

- **Respond with Presence:** Before giving advice, help, or energy, pause. Ask, "Am I offering from fullness, or from habit?"
- **Receive Without Qualification:** Practice saying "thank you" when someone offers a compliment or support, without minimizing or deflecting. Allow the energy to land. If discomfort arises, explore: "What belief am I holding about worthiness or dependence?"
- **Micro-Journaling:** Each day, use two prompts: "Where did I give today (and how did it feel)?" and "Where did I receive today (and how did I respond?)"

Dance/Flow: The Expression of Harmonic Adaptability

In Chapter 4, I wrote: "A river learns to move around the mountain rather than forcing its way through...Its current fluctuates naturally as the flow finds its way." This expression of *Wisdom* reveals how you relate to change, rhythm, and movement. It is the ability to stay attuned and responsive to life's shifts without losing your center—your grounded sense of presence. It recognizes that wisdom is not static truth, but living resonance. You don't merely react to change; you move with it. Like a dancer who adjusts to the music in real time, you remain both grounded and responsive—aware of your internal beat while attuning to the world's tempo.

When this expression is out of tune, life can feel like a series of forced movements or missed cues. You might cling to rigid routines or *go with the flow* as passive avoidance. Change is experienced as threat rather than transition. When *Harmonic Adaptability* is tuned, you maintain mental flexibility—able to pivot thoughts or strategies without resistance, you adjust with presence and move forward without losing your center, you can experience powerful emotions without clinging to them or pushing them away. Your intention remains clear, even when the path shifts. You don't just go with the flow—you *move as the flow*.

In the *4-S Process*, you: notice inflexibility or over-compliance (**Self-Discovery**), adjust to move with life's rhythms (**Self-Development**), navigate gracefully through complexity (**Self-Mastery**), and recognize that flow is living as a conscious participant in life's ongoing movement (**Self-Knowledge**).

Practice: Tuning Your Adaptability

Notice in Spirit (attention + intention) how you...

- **Practice the Pause:** Between stimulus and response, insert a moment of awareness. This brief space is where adaptability arises.
- **Use Your Body as a Barometer:** Tension in the body often signals over-control or a disconnection from flow. Where can you soften?

- **Ask for Coherence:** Ask, "Am I resisting what is, or responding to what's emerging?"
- **Practice Micro-Adjustments:** Choose small moments each day to adapt consciously, like shifting a plan when new information arises without resistance, training your system to move with, not against, the current.

Love: The Expression of Cohesive Resonance

While the faculty of Worthiness establishes *Self-Love* as our foundation, *Love* as an expression of *Wisdom* is the active principle of cohesion that restores all things to their authentic form. In chapter 8, I asked: "Is love an emotion, a force, a state of being, an act, or a morally grounded decision?" In Chapter 13, self-love was referred to as "the internal permission to treat yourself as whole and worthy of care." Imagine a transparent cube with vertex-spheres. When they drift in unexpected directions, the cube no longer looks or feels like a cube. *Love* realigns each sphere to its original location, restoring the cube to its authentic, natural form. **Love restores**. Recall the cloud in the beginning of this chapter; consider noticing the cloud as a passing illusion, and the force that anchors intention towards peace in its midst, as an *act* of love—for yourself and towards others.

Love, in this framework, is the binding resonance that unites, demystifies, and restores. It is the expression of *Wisdom* that harmonizes *Truth*, *Virtue*, *Reciprocity*, and *Flow* into a living whole. It is an energetic force of unity, clarity, and restoration; a frequency that dissolves the illusion of separation—between self and other, intention and expression, and the belief that being *you* is not enough. When tuned, *Love* expands the field of awareness and *acts on every layer of experience simultaneously*. It restores not through imposition, but through knowledge and coherence.

Where *Truth* distinguishes, *Love* unites. Where *Virtue* stabilizes, *Love* softens. Where *Reciprocity* exchanges, *Love* weaves. Where *Flow* adapts, *Love* lets go. *Love* includes others without losing the self. It allows the boundaries between giver and receiver to soften.

Without *Love*, the other expressions of *Wisdom* may function, but they lack cohesion. With *Love*, they harmonize into cohesion—a presence that breathes through all of them.

In the *4-S Process*, you: notice the cloud (**Self Discovery**), practice presence in uncertainty (**Self-Development**), choose serenity over panic (**Self-Mastery**), and recognize your resilience as the constant beneath all storms (**Self-Knowledge**).

Practice: Tuning Your Binding Resonance
Notice in Spirit (attention + intention) how you...

- **Recognize Love Not as a Transaction:** Ask, "Am I trying to be loved, or am I being love?" Consonance emerges when your presence is aligned, not when it seeks approval.
- **Create Coherence Within:** Use breath and stillness to harmonize your internal frequency. Fragmentation weakens resonance.
- **Honor Boundaries as Integrity:** Boundaries set as conscious effort to maintain alignment are not doorless walls; they are the contours of your *Authentic Self* that allow love to move freely without entanglement.
- **Let Go of Control:** Notice when the urge to fix or manage others distorts your signal. Can you remain present while letting others walk their own path?

The Interconnected Flow of Wisdom

The five expressions of Wisdom—*Truth*, *Virtue*, *Reciprocity*, *Dance/Flow*, and *Love*—do not stand alone. They are deeply interwoven in a recursive spiral. *Truth* sharpens awareness. *Virtue* gives that awareness form. *Reciprocity* applies it to relational exchange. *Dance/Flow* keeps it adaptive and attuned to timing. *Love* binds all of these into a unified resonance. This spiral is not sequential but generative; each expression amplifies the others. When all facets of *Wisdom* harmonize, you live with clarity, presence, and freedom.

The faculty of Wisdom brings our inner instruments of *Truth*, *Virtue*, *Reciprocity*, Flow, and Love into a state of beautiful, lived harmony. But what happens when we stop focusing on tuning the individual instruments and start listening to the entire orchestra as a single sound? This act of integrated listening reveals we were never isolated parts, but a unified symphony all along. This is the recognition of our own wholeness. We now turn to the faculty of *Oneness*.

CHAPTER SIXTEEN

Oneness

Oneness is not a future ideal; it is a present truth already embedded in your being. You don't need to become whole; *you already are.* This faculty reveals the capacity to remember, experience, and live from that wholeness. Unlike skills that evolve through repetition, *Oneness* is not about mastering something outside of you. It is a perceptual shift—from fragmentation to coherence. It tunes your awareness to recognize how all aspects of the self can move in concert into a unified rhythm, where contrast and difference are ingredients in a greater harmony.

Oneness doesn't erase individuality; it refines it. Each Channel of Experience—Body, Mind, Heart, and Spirit—can participate in the symphony of your life without competing for control. It is a re-integration into wholeness.

At the root of most inner conflict and relational distortion lies the perception of separation. When we forget our inherent unity, we experience disconnection from *I Am* and all its expressions, our physical experience, our mental experience, our emotional experience, our intent, our worthiness, and the inevitable relation to everything and everyone else. *Oneness* provides the lens through which life is seen as interconnected. It softens resistance and diffuses the illusion of complete separateness.

When this faculty is out of tune, fragmentation becomes the default. You may feel pulled in competing directions, stuck in "us vs. them," or overwhelmed by a world that feels scattered and adversarial. These are signals inviting you to remember that you were never truly disconnected—only unaware of the unity beneath the noise.

Recall the image from the previous chapter: the distorted cube with its displaced sphere-vertices. In the expression of *Love*, the vertices returned to their original position. The cube could now be seen again—for what it always was. *Oneness*, with *Love*, notices all its vertices, every line, its shape and form. What seemed broken or lost was never missing—only misperceived.

Integration: The Expression of Embodied Wholeness

Integration, as an expression of *Oneness*, is the continual act of including and reuniting with all the parts of yourself—especially those that have been exiled, rejected, or judged (e.g., the angry self, the uncertain self, the sensual self). It does not mean merging everything into sameness, but honoring the expressions of the *Authentic Self*. *Integration* matters because fragmentation distorts every other faculty. When you split parts of yourself into acceptable vs. unacceptable, seen vs. hidden, worthy vs. unworthy, you experience life as disjointed. When you disown parts of yourself, you weaken your ability to move with authority and autonomy. When you accept them, you restore access to your full capacity for presence and choice.

When *Integration* is out of tune, you may find yourself identifying only with certain parts (e.g., the achiever, the caregiver, the spiritual seeker), dissociating from your emotions, needs, or past experiences, or battling a subconscious belief that some part of you must be *fixed* before you can be whole; it reinforces perfection or imperfection as measuring sticks.

When tuned, *Integration* offers inner harmony, where no part of you is at war with another. Remember the principle from our exploration of experience: You are not your productivity. You are not your praise. You are not your pain. You are not your pattern. You are not even your decisions or your actions. You *are*, and every experience is always an opportunity to course-correct or reaffirm.

This expression is honed through the *4-S Process* as you notice the parts of yourself you have compartmentalized (**Self-Discovery**), develop the capacity to witness them with compassion (**Self-Development**), move as one coherent presence (**Self-Mastery**), and remember that wholeness was never lost (**Self-Knowledge**).

Practice: Tuning Your Integration

Notice in Spirit (attention + intention) how you...

- **Acknowledge Your Inner Mosaic:** Create space for every aspect of yourself to be seen without judgment: the joyful, the ashamed, the uncertain, the brave.
- **Interrupt the Fixing Reflex:** When you catch yourself trying to "improve" yourself, pause. Ask, "What if this part isn't broken, but trying to protect me or show me something I haven't yet understood?"
- **Practice Inclusive Self-Reflection:** Instead of asking, "How can I become *better*?" ask, "What part of me have I been ignoring?" Use this to create inner dialogue, not punishment. Course-correct.
- **Return to the Core:** Drop beneath your roles and stories. Sit in silence and repeat: "I am already whole. I do not need to divide myself to survive."

Balance: The Expression of Sustained Equilibrium

Balance, as an expression of *Oneness*, is the lived experience of dynamic stability. It is the ability to hold opposites without division, tension without fracture, and movement without loss of center. Whether you're navigating emotional extremes, opposing desires, or external expectations, *Balance* offers a way to stay rooted while in motion. It allows you to meet intensity without overreacting, pause without withdrawing, and change course without abandoning yourself—a state of *perceptual agility*. Life is not still; it moves and fluctuates.

Without the capacity to adapt while staying centered, we tend to rely on compensatory strategies: *over-regulation* (trying to manage everything to maintain peace while losing spontaneity) or *under-regulation* (becoming overwhelmed or destabilized by intensity, uncertainty, or perceived conflict). *Sustained Equilibrium* doesn't suppress the movement of life; it learns to dance with it. When *Balance* is out of tune, experience can feel volatile, marked by pendulum swings between extremes or a rigidity that resists change, leading to energetic drain or overexertion.

Shedding Light on Balance

Consider this: Imagine standing within a spacious room, illuminated only by a single lamp placed at one end. As you step closer toward the lamp, its radiance brightens, yet the shadow behind you grows deeper and more defined. Conversely, stepping away into the room's farther reaches shrinks your shadow—but the surrounding darkness gradually envelops you. At either extreme—immersed entirely in blinding brightness or completely in darkness—you lose the ability to see clearly. Only in the interplay of light and shadow between these extremes does clear contrast and perception emerge.

Yet balance here isn't about standing exactly at the midpoint between darkness and light. Rather, it's recognizing that the room itself is already perfectly balanced—light and dark co-existing as a whole. Your choice of where to dwell is not about correcting an imbalance, but consciously deciding which position best serves your clarity, experience, and vision.

Balance is refined through the *4-S Process* as you notice where you have over-identified with one role or emotional stance (**Self-Discovery**), practice internal flexibility (**Self-Development**), navigate movement without fear (**Self-Mastery**), and understand that *Balance* is a dynamic intelligence, not a fixed state (**Self-Knowledge**).

Practice: Tuning Your Equilibrium
Notice in Spirit (attention + intention) how you...

- **Observe Your Inner Tilt:** Take regular inventory of your inner state. Are you leaning too far into giving without receiving? Is your energy overly focused on doing, neglecting being? Naming the poles you're navigating helps you find the middle.
- **Regulate Through Breath and Posture:** Your body is the quickest tuning fork. A simple *Tri-Breath Reset*—inhaling for 4, holding for 2, exhaling for 6—sends a powerful signal to your nervous system that *Balance* is available.
- **Check for Anchoring:** Many lose balance when their center is located outside themselves—in approval, productivity, or others' stability. Ask, "Do I feel grounded in myself, or am I outsourcing my center to something unstable?"

Alignment: The Expression of Inner and Outer Congruence

Alignment is the capacity to live in harmony between *intention + attention* and your outer expression. It is the felt sense of congruence, where what you intend, believe, and value flows seamlessly into what you choose, say, and do. The reference point for alignment is your *I Am*, not external roles or feedback, nor rigid consistency with past choices—patterns that often stem from perceptual distortion. When you are aligned, integrity and authenticity become one seamless movement. Ask yourself, "Is this movement mostly inward (honoring congruence), outward (expressed integrity), or both?"

When this expression is out of tune, even simple decisions begin to feel draining. You toggle between obligations, second-guess your intuition, or defer choices altogether. Effort becomes scattered and momentum stalls; you rely on willpower rather than *the power of will*. You may feel as if *Passion* is untuned—out of sync with your *why*— when instead the deeper misalignment is with your *who*. When *Alignment* is tuned, your energy flows neatly towards intended outcomes and designed experiences, reflecting the harmony within you. Others may not always agree with your choices, but they will sense the integrity of your presence.

This expression is honed through the *4-S Process* as you: recognize misalignments between attention + intention and manifestation (**Self-Discovery**), recalibrate your choices to reflect your *I Am's* focused intention (**Self-Development**), maintain coherence under pressure (**Self-Mastery**), and trust your evolving inner compass (**Self-Knowledge**).

Practice: Tuning Your Congruence
Notice in Spirit (attention + intention) how you...

- **Inner Audit:** Before committing, ask: "Is this aligned with what I know, feel, and truly want?" Notice any resistance or false urgency.
- **Track Your Verbal Architecture**: Are you using "should" or "have to" more than "I choose" or "I value"? Language both reveals and shapes alignment—every sentence is an energetic declaration.
- **Check for Resonance:** Frequently ask, "Am I in agreement with myself right now?" This isn't a moral judgment but a gauge of inner harmony. Morality often arises from external norms or fear of judgment; Alignment arises from within.

Note: *Alignment* is the integrative product of tuned *Will* (clear direction), *Worthiness* (permission to flow), *Awareness* (perceptual accuracy), *Wisdom* (discernment), *Oneness* (connected balance), *Creativity* (adaptive expression), and *Mastery* (sustainable governance).

Synergy: The Expression of Co-Creative Flow

Synergy is the expression of *Oneness* that brings connection into motion. While *Integration*, *Balance*, and *Alignment* develop your internal unity, *Synergy* reveals what becomes possible when your inner coherence engages harmoniously with others, systems, and life itself. It is the dance of collaborating and complementing.

It honors uniqueness while uncovering a greater potential together than any part could produce alone. It's the living art of moving from consonance (fit) into resonance (mutual amplification)—not just with people, but with timing, circumstances, and emergent possibility, recognizing interconnection and activating it. *Synergy* is what happens when your clarity strengthens others and theirs amplifies your own.

When this expression is out of tune, collaborations feel dissonant or draining. You might feel you're always giving and nothing flows back, or you may resist collaboration entirely. Without synergy, even the most aligned inner life can remain isolated, and the harmony you cultivate within may never extend into the world around you.

Synergy is refined through the *4-S Process* as you notice where your efforts resonate with others (**Self-Discovery**), practice tuning into the shared field (**Self-Development**), move from isolated action to co-creative contribution (**Self-Mastery**), and recognize that synergy is about life amplifying through you and others (**Self-Knowledge**).

> Note: It's useful to distinguish *Synergy* from *Reciprocity* (see Chapter 15). *Reciprocity*, an expression of *Wisdom*, maintains harmony through attuned exchange. *Synergy*, an expression of *Oneness*, transcends exchange and moves into co-creative emergence, where the whole becomes greater than the sum of its parts.

Practice: Tuning Your Co-Creative Flow

Notice in Spirit (attention + intention) how you...

- **Anchor in Inner Clarity:** Check your internal coherence before engaging with others. Is your intention collaborative or compensatory?
- **Practice Relational Attunement:** Pay attention to timing, energy, and mutual capacity. Notice if someone is receptive before offering input. Listen to the unspoken rhythm in a conversation.

- **Release Over-Control:** Invite others' contributions to shape the process. Releasing control doesn't mean becoming passive; it means trusting the intelligence of the whole.
- **Recalibrate When Misalignment Occurs:** Pause and clarify: Is this about miscommunication, timing, or unmet needs? Ask yourself, "What's mine to carry, and what's not?"

The Interconnected Flow of Oneness

The four expressions of Oneness—*Integration*, *Balance*, *Alignment*, and *Synergy*—form a self-reinforcing spiral. *Integration* anchors inner wholeness. *Balance* sustains harmony amidst motion. *Alignment* attunes your unfiltered intent with your expression. And *Synergy* expands that unity through *shared creation*. This spiral then loops back, deepening your *Integration* as new collaborations and possibilities arise. As you tune *Oneness*, you stop seeking coherence from the outside.

The faculty of Oneness allows you to live from a place of integrated wholeness and participate in the co-creative flow of life. When you are no longer fragmented, manifestation occurs from fullness. This coherence is the very substance of the final faculty: *Creativity*.

CHAPTER SEVENTEEN

CREATIVITY

The faculty of *Creativity* is the inherent capacity through which unseen potential becomes tangible form. It is not a skill that only artists possess; it is the activated presence of possibility in motion. *Creativity* expresses itself not just through art; it *is* art through how you speak, solve, feel, think, and choose. At its core, it is the movement from the formless into form, and it is a faculty you are already using in every moment. When tuned, it transforms life into an ever-renewing field of deliberate expression.

This faculty surfaces four primary expressions, which together represent how the energy of possibility flows into lived experience:

- **Imagination:** The *instrument* that opens the entire spectrum of possibility.
- **Faith:** Infuses that potential with trust and directional energy, shifting probability toward creation.
- **Visualization:** tunes the energy into a coherent vision with intention.
- **Manifestation:** brings that vision into realized form.

To live from your creative potential, you simply expand your awareness that every breath, thought, and action is already a creation. You are not learning to *become* creative; you are realizing you always *have been*. You no longer question if you can create; *you choose what to create*.

Imagination: The Expression of Raw Potential

Imagination is the entry point to creation. It is where possibility first takes shape. Long before something manifests, it exists in this vibrational field. What you allow yourself to imagine—whether triggered consciously or unconsciously—sets the boundaries of what you can then create. *Imagination* matters because it expands your field of awareness, allowing you to explore new futures and reframe past events. Every innovation begins as an imagined possibility.

It is helpful to distinguish creativity from its cousins. **Generation**, the re-combining of existing patterns, uses existing building blocks to form recognizable outcomes, like rearranging notes in a known melody. **Regeneration** refines or reproduces those forms, as in re-playing the same melody with minor variations. **Creativity**, by contrast, emerges directly from the field of raw potential and endless possibility, untethered from familiar templates. *Imagination* is the doorway to that realm. It invites us to explore truly new configurations. In the *Flow of Existence*, imagination lights the spark; faith, visualization, and action carry it forward into form.

Fantasy is imagination unconstrained. It operates without filters, often testing extremes or bypassing practical reference points. While it may carry strong emotional tones or subconscious needs, this openness is precisely what can inspire creativity. When imagination is dismissed as *mere* fantasy, or suppressed by fear (often fear of shame or even of authenticity itself), your creative field contracts. Potential stagnates, and possibilities narrow to what was deemed as acceptable. *Fantasy* is not a problem—it is often the first sweep of signal from an undefined field. Rather than minimize it, you can recognize *fantasy* as a necessary first scan of possibility—raw, unrefined, and full of creative clues. Consider it not as the opposite of reality, but as a signal from a reality not yet structured into form.

When *Imagination* is out of tune, you may experience mental rigidity (a limited ability to see beyond current circumstances), over-identification with "realism" (mistaking *what is* for all that *can be*), fear-based speculation (looping through worst-case scenarios rather than possibility), or escapist fantasy (dwelling in imagined futures without engagement or grounding).

Imagination is honed through the *4-S Process* as you: realize that imagination is not escape—it is access to possibility (**Self-Discovery**), practice mental flexibility, open-ended inquiry, or invoking "impossible" scenarios (**Self-Development**), shape those scenarios into clear possibilities, filtering out emotional clutter (**Self-Mastery**), and recognize how your imagination reflects your evolving range of *I Am* (**Self-Knowledge**).

Practice: Tuning Your Imagination

Notice in Spirit (attention + intention) how you...

- **Pause and Expand:** Pause before trying to *figure it out*. Ask, "What else might be possible if there were no limitations or assumptions?"
- **Engage Open-Ended Imagery:** Use metaphor or abstract symbols to widen your internal field.
- **Track Vibrational Tone:** Notice how an imagined scenario *feels*. Is it heavy, chaotic, or coherent and steady? Let this resonance guide refinement.
- **Let Imagination Lead Inquiry:** Take an imagined outcome and ask, "What would have to be true for this to manifest?" Steady coherence is the sign of an in-tune imagination.

Faith: The Expression of Energized Coherence

Faith activates the movement from potential to probability. Consider it here not as passive belief, but the energetic alignment that generates momentum. While *Imagination* opens the field, *Faith* is the energetic charge that allows you to step into it. Without faith, the spark of possibility can dim under the weight of doubt. *Faith* couples your inner state to your intention through phase agreement and resonance. That resonance becomes the fuel of creation. This expression of *Faith*—the active energy of coherence—is the focused application of the foundational *Faith* we explored in Chapter 7.

When this expression is out of tune, creativity stalls. You might chase outcomes without resonance (a weak coupling to your intention), waver in doubt, attach unfounded belief to outcome—equating manifestation with validation, or mistake faith for rigid control. Tuning your *Faith* is not about eliminating uncertainty; it's about staying energetically resonant with your creative direction, even in the presence of the unknown. When *Faith* is tuned, it charges *Creativity*. You feel drawn toward your vision with calm conviction of possibility. Doubt may still visit, but it no longer defines you.

Practice: Tuning Your Faith

Notice in Spirit (attention + intention) how you...

- **Return to Resonance:** Revisit the original "yes" behind your intention. Feel it. Let its core frequency strengthen your resolve.
- **Uncouple Faith from Outcome:** Place your trust in the alignment of the process, not in a specific timeline or result.
- **Use Doubt as Data:** When doubt arises, examine what filter it reveals—fear, fatigue, or a misalignment with your true intention?
- **Engage the Body:** Move, breathe, or speak from your intention to energize it somatically and reinforce your vibrational alignment.
- **Reinforce Through Practice:** Small, coherent actions strengthen the coupling between your faith frequency and creative intent.

Visualization: The Expression of Clarified Vision

Visualization is how intention becomes image. It channels the charged potential of *Imagination* and *Faith* into an organized, coherent structure. Without a clear vision, the creative field remains potent but directionless. A clarified vision transforms the unseen into a vivid mental blueprint that guides your thoughts and actions. This internal clarity becomes an aligned framework, offering both focus and real-time feedback. When tuned, *Visualization* is not idle daydreaming; it is structural tuning. It gives the creative process its energetic architecture. Tuning *Visualization* begins by re-establishing coherence between your intention and your inner imagery.

When this expression is out of tune, your creative direction gets confused. You might have blurry or chaotic images (you can't *see* your intention coherently), a conflict between your vision and your beliefs (what you visualize feels unreachable or insincere), or a tendency to replay fear-based scenarios (habitual visualization of failure, rejection, or collapse).

This expression is honed through the *4-S Process* as you: realize that you already visualize and identify what you do (**Self-Discovery**), cultivate clear mental imagery rooted in focused intention rather than default scripts (**Self-Development**), leverage *visualization* to synchronize thoughts, emotions, and somatic states into a unified directive (**Self-Mastery**), and recognize that each image you generate reflects your filters, then consciously choose which ones to keep or release (**Self-Knowledge**).

Practice: Tuning Your Vision

Notice in Spirit (attention + intention) how you...

- **Re-center on Intent:** What is the felt reason behind your vision? Anchor the image in that clarity.
- **Use Sensory Layering:** Engage multiple senses in your mental imagery—sound, motion, emotion, texture—to deepen the coherence and resonance.
- **Release Outcome Pressure:** Let the image evolve and refine without needing it to be perfect or final.
- **Check for Interference:** Ask, "Is this image distorted by fear, comparison, or inherited filters?"

Manifestation: The Expression of Realized Form

Manifestation is the most conscious outcome of aligned energy, vision, and intent. Every experience you have is a form of creation. What shifts with awareness is how closely the result matches your professed intention. This expression matters because without it, creativity remains unrealized. Until an idea is embodied—spoken, built, or lived—it remains formless. *Manifestation* completes the creative loop, bringing form into being and offering feedback for the next cycle.

When this expression is out of tune, you may feel stuck in potential, disappointed with outcomes, or you may find yourself in a state of effort without return. These are signs that earlier intentions or filters need fresh examination. Tuning *Manifestation* means refining the conditions that allow form to emerge with integrity.

This expression is honed through the *4-S Process* as you: realize that your life is already a manifestation of prior thoughts, emotions, beliefs, and focus (**Self-Discovery**), learn to express aligned visions in tangible or relational form (**Self-Development**), deliberately fine-tune your actions and expressions so they reflect your clear intent (**Self-Mastery**), and recognize *Manifestation* as feedback—each result reflects your current tuning, not your identity (**Self-Knowledge**).

Practice: Tuning Your Manifestation

Notice in Spirit (attention + intention) how you...

- **Slow Down the Output:** Tune into the *quality*, not just the quantity, of what you're producing.
- **Revisit Upstream Phases:** If the result feels off, check the clarity of your intention, the resonance of your faith, and the coherence of your vision.
- **Honor Small Manifestations:** Celebrate alignment in a conversation, a gesture, or a moment of presence—not just in big, completed goals.

- **Let Form Surprise You:** Stay open to how the result arrives. It may differ in shape from your vision but match it in essence.

The Interconnected Flow of Creativity

The expressions of Creativity: *Imagination*, *Faith*, *Visualization*, and *Manifestation*—form a continuously cycling loop, mirroring the *Flow of Existence: From Pure Possibility to Creation/Manifestation.* They are not linear steps but dynamic resonances within a living continuum.

Imagination opens the spectrum of potential, surfacing raw, unstructured possibility. *Faith* then infuses that potential with vibrational charge and coherence, steering it toward alignment. *Visualization* translates that charged field into an organized internal blueprint, a clear architecture of intent. *Manifestation* completes the loop, collapsing that coherent energy into lived experience, where form becomes feedback and awareness expands. From that feedback, perception refines, imagination reopens, and the cycle renews itself. *Creativity is not episodic*; it's evolutionary—a continual unfolding of potential into form, guided by awareness, faith, and deliberate expression.

CHAPTER EIGHTEEN

Conclusion of the Seven Faculties

The seven *Faculties—Mastery*, *Awareness*, *Worthiness*, *Will*, *Wisdom*, *Oneness*, and *Creativity* are already alive within you, shaping your moment-to-moment experience, whether consciously expressed or unconsciously distorted. They do not activate in sequence; they work symphonically, sometimes in harmony, sometimes in dissonance. Like tuning forks within a single instrument, the Faculties harmonize or interfere depending on their tuning.

Mastery clarifies your relationship with life itself, centering your authority and autonomy, yet it cannot express cleanly unless supported by **Awareness**. *Awareness* illuminates perception, but it only deepens when guided by **Wisdom** and grounded in **Oneness**. **Worthiness** is the inner recognition that you belong, which strengthens your **Will** with confidence and empowers your **Creativity** with self-trust. *Will* directs intention into action, but it requires **Wisdom** to discern its path. *Wisdom* governs interpretation and response, sustained by *Awareness* for clarity and by *Creativity* for form. *Oneness* heals fragmentation, but it is not passivity; it is an empowered connection sustained by *Will*. Finally, *Creativity* brings it all into form, its expression an echo of your alignment—or your distortion.

This is not a fixed formula but a dynamic field. Sometimes, you act from *Will* before fully understanding your *Wisdom*. Other times, your *Awareness* awakens through the friction of misaligned *Mastery*. What matters is not sequence, but presence. The more you tune each Faculty, the more coherence you bring to your entire system.

You have now encountered these seven core Faculties as living forces to recognize. Part III has not been a curriculum of self-improvement, but an unveiling of the capacities already at play within you. It offered a chance to recognize:

- **Mastery** as the rhythm of actualizing and living.
- **Awareness** as the clarity that cuts through distortion.
- **Worthiness** as the inner recognition of belonging.
- **Will** as the force that shapes direction.
- **Wisdom** as the guide to an aligned path.
- **Oneness** as the return to undivided presence.
- **Creativity** as the form these forces take.

Each Faculty offered a distinct lens of perception, a tuning method, a deeper insight into how you shape your world, and a way to recalibrate your intention, attention, and expression. What once may have felt like many distinct ideas now reveals itself as a unified field of understanding. With Part III complete, you're not carrying more ideas—you're carrying a refined map of your inner architecture, and you have the tools to shift it at will.

Return to any Faculty to recalibrate and re-align it with ever-deeper levels of experience. You are not starting over; you are spiraling inward—each turn refining resonance. There is no final state or arrival, only ever-clearer tuning.

This completes the core conceptual journey of the book. What follows is not brand-new content, but a final act of integration—a concise weaving together of all you've encountered so far.

CHAPTER NINETEEN

FINAL INTEGRATION

Bringing All Together

As we journeyed through *BEing: The Architecture of Experience*, what you've traced is a living rhythm—the *Flow of Existence*—the ever-present movement through which consciousness expresses, learns, and renews itself.

- The Foundations provide the underlying models that orient awareness.
- The 4-S Process shows how awareness moves: discover, develop, master, and know.
- The Faculties tune your experience in real time.

Together, they map the continuous motion of perception, creation, and refinement that underlies all experience. Below is a compact map of the *Flow of Existence*, showing how awareness moves from potential to lived experience.

1. **Pure Possibility:** The non-dual, undifferentiated, infinite field of unshaped raw potential and endless possibilities

from which every experience can emerge; the non-dual ground of all existence.

2. **I Am:** The emergent self; the awakening of awareness—the recognition that you are the one who creates your experience.
3. **Intention:** *Will*, acting and selecting a subset of potentials; the directional impulse that gives movement to potential.
4. **Faculties:** Seven inherent capacities—functional *filters* and *resonators*—that refine and color the movement from Intention.
5. **Perspective & Attention:** The interpretive lens and selective focus that narrow the spectrum of potential into a specific trajectory of experience, guiding how energy *becomes* experience.
6. **Creation/Manifestation:** The tangible, observable form of expression and inner alignment—the outcome as lived form.
7. **Feedback Loop:** The reflective awareness that listens, learns, and refines the next movement (Stages 3 through 5).

Integration in Practice

You don't need to memorize these stages or treat them as steps. The *Flow of Existence* already moves through you every day. When you pause deeply before acting, that pause is the space of *Pure Possibility*. When you sense "*I Am*" before deciding, awareness arises (Stage 2). You choose a direction, so *Intention* activates (Stage 3). As you notice which *Faculty* supports that moment—perhaps Will to act, or Wisdom to discern—you are engaging your inner architecture (Stage 4). Your *Perspective and Attention* decide lens selection of focus (Stage 5), shaping *Creation/Manifestation* as lived experience (Stage 6). And every outcome, pleasant or not, becomes *Feedback* (Stage 7), returning insight to refine the next movement.

Integration is not another task. It is recognizing the process. The more consciously you participate, the more harmonious your experience becomes. Your life becomes the ongoing experience—presence, coherence, and creative freedom.

CODA

Pure Possibility is the blank score—the silent pages waiting to be filled; the endless source of every note you could ever play, every faculty already within you, every moment lived, and every outcome still forming—returning there through the *Feedback Loop*. The *Foundations* are the base from which to compose and arrange. The *Foundational Pillars* are the written notes, the structure of key, time, and tempo: *Words Do Matter*, *I Am*, *Duality and Polarity*, *Framing Your Reality*, *BFCK*, the *Four Channels of Experience*, and *Faceted BEing*. The *Faculties* are the instruments in your inner orchestra: *Mastery's* strings, *Awareness's* woodwinds, *Worthiness's* brass, *Will's* percussion, *Wisdom's* harp, *Oneness's* chorus, and *Creativity's* full ensemble improvisation. And *Spirit*, your aligned *Attention* and *Intention*, is the conductor's baton, shaping how each section enters, crescendos, and rests.

This is where the *4-S Process* guides your practice. *Self-Discovery* is the warm-up—listening to each instrument, noticing which sections are out of tune. *Self-Development* is the rehearsal—practicing passages, refining dynamics, and learning to play in harmony. *Self-Mastery* is the performance under pressure, holding your part with poise. And *Self-Knowledge* is the live concert—embodying the full score and feeling the resonance of every note within you.

No symphony stays the same. Each performance informs the next. A subtle shift in *attention* here, a deeper sense of *worthiness* there, a new riff of *creativity*, a fresh modulation of *wisdom*. The loop of creation continues: *imagination* inspires *faith*, faith shapes *vision*, vision brings form, and that form provides *feedback* to imagine again.

The baton is in your hand. You are both the composer and the conductor of your life's symphony. The *Foundations Pillars* have given you the score, the *Faculties* have supplied your instruments, and the *4-S Process* has guided your engagement. Now, you step onto the stage of each moment:

- **Listen** (Self-Discovery) for the notes that are out of tune.
- **Practice** (Self-Development) where your playing feels uncertain.
- **Play** (Self-Mastery) with full presence, whatever the acoustics or audience.
- **Reflect** (Self-Knowledge) on the resonance of the music you create—and let that inform your next composition.

When you set this book down, keep in mind: others will play their melody nearby. Some may invite you into their rhythm; others will ask that you follow their lead. Yet the gesture of direction remains yours. You are the sole conductor of your own orchestra. Only you can set the tone, the rhythm, and the texture of your expression. The choice is always yours: to co-create within another's score or to compose your own.

This is not a test of perfection. It is composition, rehearsal, performance, and improvisation all at once. There is a difference between playing a misread piece from someone else and performing your own masterpiece from unimpeded, unconditioned authentic expression. Every gesture you make draws the Faculties into coherence, summoning the music only you can play. There will be missed cues, unexpected key changes, and strings that go out of tune. These are not failures but part of orchestration.

A masterful conductor does not worry about being misunderstood or mislabeled; their focus remains on coherence—on the clarity of the score coming through. The conductor does not fear dissonance but uses it to create tension and release, knowing that beauty often emerges through contrast and resolution. The focus is not on avoiding error, but on returning, again and again, to the resonance of your *Authentic Self*.

Your orchestra is ready. The music is yours to bring forth. And when you dance with others, listen for the beat that calls you forward, practice in tandem with each melody, dance with full presence through life's crescendos and pauses, and reflect on how your dance transformed the experience, informing the next one. You were never broken; nothing was ever missing. Write your score from the boundless field of *Pure Potential* and *Pure Possibility*. Play with the fullness of Freedom and Worthiness.

Live free. Imagine. Create. Play.
Dance to the tune of life.

Appendix A: Analogies

Throughout this book, we have used metaphor as a bridge between the unseen *Architecture of Experience* and its lived expression. The following analogies extend that bridge into familiar territory, translating the *Flow of Existence* into images you can visualize, test, and remember. Each one reveals how *Pure Possibility* becomes experience—how awareness, intention, and faculty tuning shape what takes form.

From quantum parallels to daily metaphors, these illustrations invite you to see the creative process not as abstraction, but as a living dialogue between perception and participation.

Double-Slit Parallel

A. The Quantum Setup

Electrons go through two slits and hit a screen. If no which-path information is recorded, a fringe pattern appears (coherence preserved). If path information is recorded (by any interaction), fringes vanish (decoherence). It's the physical encoding of path info—not "looking"—that changes the outcome.

B. Flow Mapping

- **Stage 5 — Perspective & Attention (Lens + Aim):**
  In *Flow of Existence* terms, you set the **lens** (what the apparatus allows to remain coherent) and the **aim** (what you actually condition/read out). Practically, this means choosing a configuration that either **preserves** or **marks**

which-path information, and choosing **how** you'll read the results.

- **Stage 6 — Creation/Manifestation (Formed Outcome):**
  The **pattern on the screen**—fringes or no fringes—emerges from many localized hits. This is the lived result of the conditions you established and the signals you chose to register.
- **Stage 7 — Feedback:**
  You adjust future setups and readouts based on what appeared—tightening isolation if you want coherence, or deliberately marking paths if you need particle-like outcomes.

C. Flow Insight (why intention alone isn't enough)

Wanting fringes (intention) won't produce them if the setup or readout leaks path information. To realize a "wave-like" outcome, it is necessary that Stage 5 aligns both the **lens** (coherence-friendly design) and the **aim** (non-path-conditioning readout). Then **Stage 6** manifests the corresponding pattern.

Stage 5 sets what can stay coherent and what will be read; Stage 6 shows you the pattern you've made possible.

White-Light Through Colored Lenses

A. Optics (clean phrasing)

White light contains many wavelengths. A red filter *transmits* a band near red and *attenuates* others. An aperture/polarizer then sets *how much* light passes and (optionally) *orientation*.

B. Flow Mapping (with Stage 5 combined)

- Stage 5 — Perspective & Attention (Lens + Aim):
  Perspective works like the spectral filter—beliefs, assumptions, and emotional tone determine which "bands" of possibility can pass.
  Attention is the **aperture/polarizer**—it sets *how much* of the filtered signal you let through and (if relevant) the orientation you select.

In the *Flow of Existence*, these operate as one linked stage: your **lens** (what can pass) and your **aim** (what you actively admit) together determine the signal that reaches experience.

- Stage 6 — Creation/Manifestation (Formed Outcome): The "image" that appears—broadband clarity or intentional coloration—is the outcome of the filter you set and the aperture you chose.

C. Faculty-Level Tuning (kept practical)

- **Worthiness** widens/neutralizes the filter so options once excluded ("undeserved") can transmit.
- **Wisdom** discerns which filters **clarify** (reduce noise/bias) and which **distort** (over-attenuate valuable bands).

Stage 5 chooses the spectrum and the dose; Stage 6 is the picture that forms from what you let through.

Quick side-by-side

Flow Stage	Double-Slit	White-Light
5. Perspective & Attention	Set apparatus for coherence or path-marking **and** choose readout/conditioning	Set spectral filter (**Perspective**) and aperture/polarizer (**Attention**)
6. Creation / Manifestation	Pattern on screen (fringes vs. bands) from accumulated hits	Formed image: broadband clarity or intentional coloration
7. Feedback	Re-tune isolation/marking to align with desired outcome	Re-tune filters/aperture to align clarity or hue with intention

Notes

- This is **not** a claim that consciousness alters quantum outcomes. The analogies show how **setup + readout** (Stage 5) determines the **pattern** (Stage 6).
- *Perspective & Attention* as **one stage** fits both analogies: lens+aim in optics, design+readout in the slit experiment.
- The metaphors remain **quantum-inspired** and **optics-accurate**.

The Alchemist's Kitchen (Culinary Parallel)

How the Flow of Existence appears through the act of creation.

Imagine entering a kitchen where every ingredient, tool, and source of heat mirrors a stage of the *Flow of Existence*.

Flow Stage	Culinary Parallel	Description
1 – Pure Possibility	The open pantry	You open your pantry and find every ingredient imaginable—an undifferentiated field of culinary potential. Nothing has been selected or shaped. This is Pure Possibility, the open canvas before any intention arises.
2 – I Am	The Chef's presence	You step forward as the Chef—awareness entering the space. Your intuition, preferences, and readiness meet the kitchen. The "I Am" becomes the one who will shape what follows.
3 – Intention	Choosing the dish	You decide: ***"I'm making a stew that nourishes, surprises, and bridges sweet, savory, and bright notes."*** Intention becomes the guiding vector for every choice, the directional impulse that gives motion to potential.
4 – Faculties	Seven alchemical tools	Each Faculty functions as a transmutation force that shapes how Intention takes form: • **Mastery – Structure**: workflow, order, sequencing, mise en place. • **Awareness – Sensory Feedback**: tasting, smelling, noticing subtle shifts. • **Worthiness – Ingredient Quality**: honoring the value of each ingredient; not collapsing into scarcity when quality matters. • **Will – Heat Source**: consistent simmering, disciplined stirring, patience that prevents scorches or rush. • **Wisdom – Discernment**: Distinguishing nuances of salt, acid, fat, and sweetness; the knowing of when refinement is complete. • **Oneness – Integration**: blending, emulsifying, layering elements into coherence. • **Creativity – Novelty**: introducing unexpected pairings and finishing gestures—herb oil, citrus zest, textures that elevate the whole. These tools do not act separately. Their combined modulation tunes the unfolding experience.

Flow Stage	Culinary Parallel	Description
5 – Perspective & Attention	Lens and focus	• **Perspective (Lens)**: You choose the cuisine frame—perhaps Mediterranean heartiness with Asian brightness. • **Attention (Focus)**: You track the variables that bring that lens to life: the heat curve, reduction point, timing, and textural checkpoints. These shape where experience narrows and how potential becomes form.
6 – Creation / Manifestation	The Stew	The rich, multi-layered dish emerges. Guests taste earthy umami, bright acidity, and sweet root notes, and they feel nourished. Manifestation here is not random; it's the coherence of all prior stages. The form taken by your sequence of choices.
7 – Feedback Loop	Tasting and refinement	Feedback clarifies alignment or distortion, inviting refinement. You offer a trusted friend a taste. "Needs more brightness," or "A bit too salty." These serve as data. You then: • **Notice** the gap between your intention and the experience. • **Diagnose** which Faculty may have been out of tune—Awareness missing a late salt rise, Wisdom overbalancing, Will rushing reduction, Worthiness compromising quality. • **Retune Stage 5** through a shift in Perspective (leaning brighter) and Attention (monitoring reduction more closely). • **Re-manifest**: add lemon or vinegar, adjust heat, re-emulsify—then serve again. Each iteration refines coherence.

Just as a memorable dish depends on tuned flavor, timing, and texture, your lived experience depends on attuned Faculties, clear Intention, and focused Attention. Every cycle of tasting, refining, and re-serving echoes the *Flow of Existence*: experience becomes data, data becomes wisdom, and wisdom renews intention.

Appendix B: The Symphony of the Faculties - Instrument Rationale

In the CODA, the seven faculties are presented as sections of an orchestra. Here is the rationale for each pairing.

The Instrument	The Faculty & Rationale
Strings	**Mastery:** Strings—violins, violas, cellos, and basses—form the backbone of most orchestral textures, capable of both powerful, sustained tones and subtle, precise articulations. This mirrors Mastery's role: providing a stable yet flexible foundation and shaping the "tonal center" of your life with both strength and nuance.
Woodwinds	**Awareness:** Woodwinds (flutes, clarinets, oboes) bring clarity, color, and the ability to "speak" with a highly attentive quality. They cut through dense textures with their timbral brightness, just as Awareness illuminates and distinguishes the finer details of experience.
Brass	**Worthiness:** Brass instruments (trumpets, horns, trombones) convey confidence, warmth, and a poised projection. They declare presence boldly and carry the "noble" harmonies that underpin a piece. This aligns with Worthiness: the inner sense of value that gives your life its dignified, unshakeable resonance.
Percussion	**Will:** Percussion provides pulse, momentum, and rhythmic structure—the driving energy that keeps movement alive. It marks beginnings, accents, and momentum. Will is that very directional force, keeping you on beat, initiating movement, and sustaining focus.

The Instrument	The Faculty & Rationale
Harp	**Wisdom:** The harp's plucked strings evoke both delicate insight and a gentle, unfolding clarity. Its resonance suggests reflection and harmonic richness, qualities of Wisdom as it discerns, guides, and weaves meaning through complexity.
Chorus	**Oneness:** A chorus brings many voices into a single, unified sound. It's the ultimate image of parts dissolving into a harmonious whole. Oneness, likewise, celebrates individual expressions while revealing their interdependence in a cohesive field.
Improvisation	**Creativity:** Creativity is the spark that generates the new. It is not limited to one section; it arises as a full ensemble improvisation, introducing fresh motifs, unexpected variations, and novel expressions that transform the score from a static plan into living art.

The Conductor's Baton: Spirit (attention + intention)

The conductor's baton guides how, when, and with what intensity each section enters—ensuring all voices move in dynamic alignment.

www.ingramcontent.com/pod-product-compliance
Lightning Source LLC
LaVergne TN
LVHW090602110826
845146LV00001B/225

* 9 7 9 8 9 9 4 5 3 7 2 0 6 *